DESTINY ENCOUNTER

Andrew Rabontsi Motsilanyane

authorHOUSE®

AuthorHouse™ UK Ltd.
1663 Liberty Drive
Bloomington, IN 47403 USA
www.authorhouse.co.uk
Phone: 0800.197.4150

Published by AuthorHouse 08/19/2014

ISBN: 978-1-4969-8436-4 (sc)
ISBN: 978-1-4969-8434-0 (hc)
ISBN: 978-1-4969-8435-7 (e)

Dedication

This book is dedicated to the King of kings, my Lord and Saviour Jesus Christ, whom has shown me grace in all areas of my life. I would also like to dedicate this book to my Family and all my brothers and sisters in Christ and many other thousands of people who will be enlightened by its message.

Contents

Acknowledgment

I would like to take this opportunity to express my sincere gratitude to the Holy God, my Father, whom I Love with all of my heart. Thank you for using me as your mouth piece in this project and conveying your message, through this book: Destiny Encounter.

Apostle Kingsley Ohene-Marfo and the Victory Celebration Center family, Thank you for giving me a voice and a platform in church to exercise my knowledge and capabilities, I am very grateful.

My beautiful wife, Thank you for being a pillar of support throughout this project and many other projects we had together. May the Lord richly increase you from glory to glory.

My mother, Ms Pelegamotse Girly Motsilanyane, I am always speechless when I remember the numerous occasions the Lord had used you, together with my late father, to show me the right way of life, without you giving up on me. Thank you and may the Lord continue to guard and guide you in all that you do in order to fulfill your divine assignment here on earth.

To Ms Eva Maria Lekhonkhobe. The Lord gave you a vision of this book. You believed in it and instigated it through prayer. Thank you for your inspirational words and your encouragement, may the Lord increase you in every aspect of your life.

To Mr Seliki and Ms Thapelo Tlhabane. Your involvement in my life is overwhelming. May the Lord of grace increase the wisdom that you carry in order to impact your generation positively. I Thank you for all those years you've given me counsel.

Katlego and Neo my siblings, I truly appreciate your involvement and the inputs you have made in this project, you are indeed a blessing in our lives. Receive a special grace, from the Lord, to excel in all your endeavors.

My son Bobo, you are destined for greatness. May the Lord give you grace to serve Him all the days of your life.

My beautiful nieces, Masego and Kamogelo. May the favor of the most high God rest upon you throughout your lives.

Professor Eno Ebenso, Thank you for being a good inspirational supervisor. I am grateful of your involvement towards my academic endeavour.

Special gratitude also goes to, Rulers Palace under the leadership of Prophet Elijah Agyei. It's not long that we are together and yet I could see the manifestation of God's glory; Surely, The Lord has set aside a massive assignment for us, for His Name to be Glorified.

AuthorHouse team, Hannah, April, Jay, Merly, Sarah, Rey, Lisa, Vanessa and Jan. I have learned a lot from you guys. Thank you for doing this explicit work for us. I really appreciate you all.

How can I not thank my dear friends, special colleagues and extended family members who are contributing to my life; Mr Richard and Ms Stella Motsilanyane, and Men and women of God who assisted me on this project, I thank you.

My Grandma's Mathilda Lebethe and Elizabeth Motsilanyane, I thank God for your long lives, you are a blessing.

To my late father, Mr Samuel Motsilanyane... "heaven is where he is... Thank you Jesus..."

Last but not least, my audience. For you just to have a glance of this book, makes it an immense honor to me. May the spirit of the Lord manifest itself with proof as you read through and be blessed by the words of our Lord and Savior, Jesus Christ... Let us meet at the top!

It is due to space that I can't mention other brethren by name... God has your reward, Thank you.

Love you all!

Papi

Introduction

Jeremiah 10:23: *"I know, O Lord, that the way of man is not in himself, that it is not in man who walks to direct his steps."*

The first thing we should all do before beginning to plan our destinies is to acknowledge that where we want to get in life is not in ourselves. It is not our abilities that make us who we are, what we have achieved, or even how we get to where we want to be in life. Man is not the master of his own destiny.

Every step you take is an opportunity offered to you by the Lord. Even though you are the one living your own life, for yourself, the Bible says you are not the master of it. You don't carry the access code to your future; you even need help to pursue your earthly mandate. It sounds strange, but it's the truth: you don't master your life! No matter how hard you try, you won't succeed!

Your steps are ordered and numbered by the Lord. The paths along which the Lord leads you are sometimes not desirable to walk on, but they are all good for you, and they are worth it. They are relevant, and they are rightfully made and designed to take you to your assignment in the kingdom of God, here on earth.

One man in the Bible thought he was running away from the paths ordained for him; little did he know that, even as he ran away, he was entering into the totality of the purpose of the Lord for his life. The more he ran from the Lord, the more he fulfilled and accomplished His purpose.

He lived in the belly of a fish for three days, and in the midst of everything, he experienced the Lord's miracle. His running was part of the plan for his life. He did not know that God wanted the people in the ship to experience His might through him. His running ultimately became a blessing to the people in the ship, for the glory of the Lord was revealed in their midst.

Psalm 3:8: *"Salvation belongs unto the Lord; your blessing be on your people! Selah."*

No situation is bad when the Lord is leading your life. There is no hopelessness when the Lord is in control of your steps. Even when you are in deep fear, it all fits well into the strategies of the Lord over your life.

Jeremiah 10:23: *"It is not man who walks to direct his steps."*

The word *direct* refers to a direct route, and that implies the shortest way, without turning or stopping—no roundabout …a straight, uninterrupted route.

We sometimes think that the route we travel in life is long and full of agony. We think it moves up and about without a clear definite description, and we think there is no one on the other side to hand over to us the crown of victory, complimenting us on our work well done.

Well, that's not true. In fact, when you travel with the Lord, as He directs your steps, the route to your destiny is shortened. In other words, what you were supposed to achieve in a longer period will be yours in a shorter time. Your route has no roundabouts. The Lord has carefully calculated the resultant force, which is the best and shortest distance between where you are and where you are heading. This route has no turning; it's the best possible and the straightest, shortest distance between any two points. Your interruptions are part of a strategic plan to prepare you for your next hurdle. They are part of the story that the Lord is writing about you. The Lord will take you there safely and well equipped for you to be the Joseph of your time. You will be perfect and complete, lacking in nothing as God shows you the way to prosper.

As you prosper, your surroundings should prosper as well. Those negative and unproductive surroundings will have no choice but to bear fruits for you.

Chapter 1

THE REDEMPTION

Your purpose and your mandate on earth was threatened before you were even born. Rituals were done on your behalf, and spells of evil were spoken to oppose your destiny. The world did not give you a chance for you to exist or for you to fulfill God's mandate.

Genesis 3 speaks of the curses spoken by God to Adam, Eve, and their surroundings, making it too hard for them to be productive in their land. One thing you should know is that, even when you are blessed and your surroundings are cursed, you will never make a strong impact upon the world around you, for your surroundings carry your solution. The people you work with are carrying something that will upgrade you. Your family members have the resources that will assist and guide you to greater heights. The community where you live—even that rural and remote area—has your breakthrough in it.

Maybe all these things that surround you are not encouraging and do not strengthen you. They are, in fact, casting your potential down. They hinder and disqualify you. The very same community does not want to associate with you. Your family despises your talents, and at work you are just an ordinary employee despite your contributions. It is here that you should understand and realize that what is in you is greater than that which is in the world (1 John 4:4).

James 1:2–4: *"Count it all joy, my brothers, when you meet trials of various kinds, for you know that the testing of your faith produces steadfastness. And let steadfastness have its full effect, that you may be perfect and complete, lacking in nothing."*

Genesis 2:19: *"Now out of the ground the Lord God had formed every beast of the field and every bird of the heavens and brought them to the man to see what he would call them.*

Your ground carries something special for you, and that makes it your territory, a place you should dominate. Do not be intimidated by the beasts that are presented to you by life. Neither be intimidated by their stature when they begin to threaten you when they come closer to you. The Lord is presenting them to you so you can just look upon them and wonder what you would call each and every one of them.

Most of us panic when we come across intimidating life experiences. Do not forget that *"Christ in you, the hope of glory"* (Colossians 1:27).

Just allow God to be the one presenting these things to you; don't go after them yourself. God will not present something to you that you won't be able to identify, name, and call forth. We are able to conquer all things that are brought before us by our surroundings and life in general. Be like Adam. Call and name any situation as you want it to be. Talk to your conditions, and they will respond to what you call them.

Now God spoke a curse in the Garden of Eden. A curse is a spoken word calling down evil on someone or something. Before God could call upon the curses at the Garden of Eden, He said to the woman, *"What is this that you have done?"* (Genesis 3:13).

Why did God ask Eve what she had done, when God Himself was in a rightful position to tell her what she has done? He is God. Was He not supposed to tell Eve what she had done? On the other hand, Eve had no idea of the importance of what she had just done. She was clueless. She thought she had just innocently eaten a fruit from the garden. Eve did not have eyes to see into the future, but God saw the entire human journey to eternity. God asked Eve that question not because Eve had the answer. Eve knew nothing! She did not know that she had allowed all of us today, and many others on earth in the past and future, to be born into a world of sin … a world of great anguish that will introduce us all into an era of the lost … an era of man searching for hope and many led to a complete doom to eternal darkness. God saw all of that coming to all of humanity and to all nations here on earth, and He felt the pain of man at that particular moment at the Garden.

Anger fumed out of His nostrils, and immediately God called down evil on everything and everyone who had taken part in that act of disobedience. Along the destiny of mankind, the child was born.

Isaiah 9:6: *"For to us a child is born, to us a son is given; and the government shall be upon his shoulder, and his name shall be called Wonderful Counselor, Mighty God, Everlasting Father, Prince of Peace."*

It was for this reason that Christ was born; to redeem all humanity from darkness and curses spoken by the Lord in the Garden of Eden. This was to set man free and give him access to His eternal glory.

Ephesians 1:7: *"In Him we have redemption through his blood, the forgiveness of our trespasses, according to the riches of His grace."*

Christ delivered us from sin and all penalties including those spoken by God in Eden. Whatever the magnitude of the offence, we were atoned and bought back at a price.

Jesus Redeemed Us from the Battle

The first curse was spoken by God, to the serpent.

Genesis 3:14–15: *"The Lord God said to the serpent, 'Because you have done this, cursed are you above all livestock and above all beasts of the field; on your belly you shall go, and dust you shall eat all the days of your life. I will put enmity between you and the woman, and between your offspring and her offspring.'"*

3

Matthew 1:20–21: *"For that which is conceived in her is from the Holy Spirit. She will bear a son, and you shall call his name Jesus, for he will save his people from their sins."*

The mother of Jesus conceived, and Jesus was her offspring. And on the other hand, the serpent gave forth offspring in his likeness—the demonic offspring that were ordained to enter into battle with what the woman bears (1 John 3:10).

The woman did not only give birth to a son, but she gave birth to a son who had a different mandate …a mandate to uproot and destroy the foundations of the battle between the seed of a woman and the seed of the devil.

Before Christ was born, the battle between the offspring of women and the offspring of serpents gave the devil an upper hand over mankind. Man was vulnerable and without purpose, longing for a deliverer. In the Old Testament times, before Christ was born, it was most likely for God's people to be conquered in battles by the enemy, for they fell easily to temptation, and they wavered. They did this because they were weak and did not have someone who would stand up and act on their behalf to redeem their sins permanently.

Kings failed drastically in their search for holiness, and priests could not perform their priestly duties on behalf of the people, since they themselves were weak and vulnerable to sin. Hence, Jesus became a different offspring born to a woman to redeem man from the powers of sin.

Hebrews 4:15: *"For we do not have a high priest who is unable to sympathize with our weaknesses, but one who in every respect has been tempted as we are, yet without sin."*

We have to understand that being set free from sin enables us to fight the enemy with courage.

First Kings 8:33: *"Your people Israel are defeated before the enemy because they have sinned against you."*

The devil knows this part of the scripture very well. He knows that whenever he enters into battle with those who have sinned, God's defense of them is not guaranteed. The strategies of the devil revolve around this basic principle: making God's people sin before launching into battle with them. He knows that sin will make us doubt the very gospel that is the sword of a believer (Ephesians 6:17).

Luke 5:5: *"And Simon answered, 'Master, we toiled all night and took nothing! But at your word I will let down the nets!'"*

The word of God builds faith.

Psalm 91:4: *"His faithfulness is a shield and buckler."* God became faithful to you because you have faith in Him. Your faith in Him in battles acts as a shield that protects you so that there can be no arrow that will pursue its cause against your life or the lives of the people in your family. The word of God builds this faith.

God says in Isaiah 41:10: *"Fear not, for I am with you."*

When you know you have sinned against the Lord and do not take time to reconcile with your Master, how then can you say, as Simon said, *"But at your word I will let down the nets?"* Simon was acting on faith; that is, when he says "I will," he is promising to do something because Jesus has spoken. You must act on what the Lord had said.

Sin will cloud your spirit with fear and will hinder your steps of faith. You will doubt the very weapons God has given to you for battle, which are his word, and confidence of the saints. Sin makes the glory of the Lord depart from you. It disfigures your garments and your appearance as you go into battle. It proclaims defeat.

Hebrews 2:7: *"You have crowned him with glory and honor."*

Hebrews 2:10: *"For it was fitting that he, for whom and by whom all things exist, in bringing many sons to glory, should make the founder of their salvation perfect through suffering."*

In your suffering and distress, the glory of the Lord should not depart from you as a son or daughter of the most-high God. When the devil comes with his schemes, do whatever you can to keep and maintain God's glory and power, for the Bible says, in Hebrews 1:3, *"He is the radiance of the glory of God and the exact imprint of his nature, and he upholds the universe by the word of his power."* In order for you to be able to conquer the devil, you should live a sin-free life through the blood of Jesus Christ and continue to speak the word of faith in your circumstances, which is the power of God.

First Kings 8:33–34: *"And if they turn again to you and acknowledge your name and pray and plead with you in this house, then hear in heaven and forgive the sin of your people Israel and bring them again to the land that you gave to their fathers."*

Acknowledge the offspring, whose name is Jesus, born of a woman to conquer evil and to redeem our souls from the warfare of evil … an offspring who came to crush and put to an end all schemes of darkness, in order to bring man to his rightful position.

Jesus Redeemed the Woman

Genesis 3:16: *"To the woman he said, 'I will surely multiply your pain in childbearing; in pain you shall bring forth children.'"*

The word *multiply* means "to increase." To Eve it meant that the pain during childbirth would be excessive. This also implied that, in her productivity, she should remember that she had sinned against God. This pain was supposed to remind her of the sin she had committed. This experience stood out whenever she had to receive a gift—a child she would have a strong attachment to for the entire life.

This curse has a strong impact upon everyone, male and female, to the extent that, whatever they want to bear, should come forth in pain.

First Chronicles 4:9: *"Jabez was more honorable than his brothers; and his mother called his name Jabez, saying, 'Because I bore him in pain.'"*

Here was a woman who confessed to bearing her child in pain. She testified to the fact that she bore her child in pain by naming him Jabez, a name that means "sorrow" or "trouble." This woman had given birth to other children before Jabez. What made her then associate this one with pain? But to Jabez, his name became a platform for him to access his divine purpose from God. Jabez affirmed that pain is transferable from those who experience it into those who are associated with it. But because Jabez carried this understanding, he had intentions to dissociate himself from this name.

The curse of his mother became transferable to him. She experienced a physical pain and transferred an emotional pain to her son, Jabez, because of what she had gone through. First Chronicles 4:10: *"Jabez called upon God of Israel ..."*

Note what Jabez does: he calls to the commander of curses. He does not go to his mother to question her about the name she gave to him. He knew that going to his mother would not provide any meaningful solution, since his mother herself had not had a divine revelation about what she had gone through. Jabez knew that his mother did not understand the magnitude of the curse and the extent to which it had manifested, which caused her to give him such a name.

Most often in our lives we tend to seek help from people who, according to us, are capable of taking certain burdens out of our lives. We do this thinking that they are linked one way or another to our solutions simply because they have experienced similar things to what we are going through. Rather, Jabez sought his solution from the one who carries all things in the palm of His hand. Going to people will not help. Those who need healing should call upon Him. Do you need a job? don't blame your upbringing. Don't blame your community or your family. Do one thing for yourself—call upon God. You need children? Call on Him. Your wife or your husband is not the one having the troubles in conceiving a child. Children are the fruit of the womb from God (Psalm 127:3).

In Genesis 30:1–2 we see that Rachel envied her sister when she herself bore Jacob no children. She said to Jacob, *"Give me children, or I shall die!"* Jacob's anger was kindled against Rachel, and he said, *"Am I in the place of God, who has withheld from you the fruit of the womb?"*

When we encounter marital challenges, whom do we seek advice from? Do we still remember that God is the founder of our marriage? (Mark 10:6–9). Rachel did not speak like Jabez did. She did not have an understanding of her affairs, and that is what ultimately made Jacob respond the way he did. Rachel thought Jacob was the one who should make it possible for them to bear the fruit of the womb. On the other hand, Jacob had the same revelation Jabez had. They both saw God as a resolver of man's affairs. Jacob knew that the fault was not in him or his wife.

Now Jabez called upon God.

First Chronicles 4:10: *"Oh that you would bless me and enlarge my border, and that your hand might be with me, and that you would keep me from harm so that it might not bring me pain."*

God cursed Eve. Now why then did Jabez ask God to prevent pain from coming to him? He was not a childbearer. This is because the pain was going to protrude into his life. Pain would follow him in everything he did, because of his name. Wherever he went, he would cause pain. He would cause pain to his family and colleagues, living up to his name, *"I bore him in pain"* (1 Chronicles 4:9).

Jabez refused to be limited by his name. He pronounced blessing over his life and his surroundings. He invited the hand of God upon his life against those who would plan to cause him pain.

Isaiah 66:7–8: *"Before she was in labor she gave birth; before her pain came upon her she delivered a son. Who has heard such a thing? Who has seen such things?"*

The woman spoken about is set free from a curse. She received a miracle and favor from the Lord. The prophet Isaiah marvels at what he sees and hears in the spirit. By looking at this woman who delivers before her pain comes, he understands that a law has been broken and a curse that has existed from the beginning has been brought to an end. *"Who has seen such things?"* You received your child without any pain. *"Who has heard such a thing?"* You were destined for failure, but what we see is success. Your borders were close to you; in other words, you were limited. But now you will expand!

Who is this child who is born without a mother's pain? And who is this mother who gives birth to the child without pain?

Isaiah 66:10: *"Rejoice ye with Jerusalem, and be glad for her."*

Isaiah 9:6: *"For unto us a child is born, to us a son is given."*

Through this child all pains have ceased.

Revelation 21:4: *"He will wipe away every tear from their eyes, and death shall be no more, neither shall their mourning, nor crying, nor pain anymore, for the former things have passed away."*

All pain has been cast away. Jesus came to redeem all women from the curse spoken unto them in the Garden of Eden. It is possible for the grace of God to fall upon you, and for you to become like the woman spoken about in Isaiah 66:7. Receive that word and keep it in your heart. Claim your victory through Jesus Christ. You are redeemed from the pain of childbearing. You are set free! It is possible through Him who came to redeem you from all curses.

In Galatians 3:13 we read that Christ redeemed us from the curse of the law by becoming a curse for us, but which curse is the Bible referring to? Which curse are we redeemed from? All curses. Christ has made all curses into a curse He came to redeem us from. All curses that have been written about are part of the law, and in Christ there is no law (Galatians 5:22–23)

Man and His Grounds Were Redeemed

Genesis 3:17: *"And to Adam he said, 'Because you have listened to the voice of your wife and have eaten of the tree of which I commanded you, "You shall not eat of it," cursed is the ground because of you; in pain you shall eat of it all the days of your life.'"*

Adam committed a serious mistake by listening to any voice other than that of the Lord.

John 10:3: *"To him the gatekeeper opens. The sheep hear his voice, and he calls his own sheep by name and leads them."*

Genesis 3:8: *"And they heard the sound of the Lord God walking in the garden in the cool of the day, and the man and his wife hid themselves from the presence of the Lord God among the trees of the garden. But the Lord God called to the man and said to him, 'Where are you?' And he said, 'I heard a sound of you in the garden, and I was afraid, because I was naked, and I hid myself.'"*

In the midst of all confusion and disobedience, God called Adam, and Adam responded. Sometimes when we have done wrong against the Lord, we try by all means to hide from Him when He calls. We can clearly tell that it is His voice calling, despite our nakedness. Before Adam sinned, he was very intimate with God, to the extent that he knew Him as he walked around the garden. Even after he had sinned, Adam could hear the sound of the Lord from a distance. This is what most of the believers ignore; they think that because they have sinned they will be unable to hear the Lord when He calls them into fellowship.

When you have sinned, the very same thing happens; but some people suppress and ignore the very voice they are used to—the voice of God. The fact that you are no longer well positioned in God's garden does not mean that you will be unable to hear Him when He calls. The Lord's voice is always audible to man's spirit, even to the deepest sinners. And even in your attempt to close your ears, you will always hear Him as He walks and calls you to repentance. You are never erased from His thoughts, and He will definitely come for you.

Genesis 2:190: *"Now out of the ground the Lord God had formed every beast of the field and every bird of the heavens and brought them to the man to see what he would call them. And whatever the man called every living creature, that was its name."*

Then man gave names to all livestock and to the birds of the heavens and to every beast of the field.

From the ground, God formed all things, living creatures, livestock, and seeds. Genesis 2:15: *"The Lord God took the man and put him in the garden of Eden to work it and keep it."*

Before Adam was cursed, he was supposed to work and keep the garden. Understand that, when you work, you are not under a curse. In fact, to work is a blessing. What then made the difference between the work Adam was assigned and the curse he received from God is that, after he was cursed, Adam had to work in pain. The work suddenly became more difficult. He worked in an unproductive environment. But before, everything had been productive, and he had harvested plenty. Genesis 3:17: *"In pain you shall eat of it."*

What made Adam work harder was, of course, the ground the Lord had cursed. It began to be unproductive, and Adam harvested very little. There were lots of thorns and thistles that choked the crops he sowed. The ground became harder, which made it difficult for seeds to germinate. Adam had to work on it more in order for the seeds to survive.

Are you in such a condition—working hard in unproductive ground, working in painful, hard, and harsh conditions having very little profit to show, just like Adam?

Does the ground reject your seeds? Are they choked so that they don't survive? Have some that have managed to grow become trees that do not bear a single fruit, after you have wasted so much on them?

Matthew 21:18–19: *"In the morning, as He [Jesus] was returning to the city, he became hungry. And seeing a fig tree by the wayside, he went to it and found nothing on it but only leaves. And He said to it, 'May no fruit ever come from you again!'"*

Do we blame the tree or the ground? What does the Bible say? Does it not say that the ground was cursed? The poor fig tree grew in a cursed environment, and it was therefore associated with a curse. It became like many other trees that failed to bear fruit, even if they looked as if something good would come out of them.

Our ground does not only carry our possession, but it is our possession for wealth. God formed everything from the ground, and treasures are placed in it, so attract your blessings from it. Your ground is a special place through which you can access your excess.

Genesis 6:1–6: *"When man began to multiply on the face of the land and daughters were born to them, the sons of God saw that the daughters of man were attractive. And they took as their wives any they chose. Then the Lord said, 'my spirit shall not abide in man forever, for he is flesh: his days shall be 120 years.' The Nephilim were on the earth in those days, and also afterward, when the sons of God come in to the daughters of man and bore children to them. These were the mighty who were men of old, the men of renown. The Lord saw that the wickedness of man was great in the earth, and that every intention of the thoughts of his heart was only evil continually. And the Lord was sorry that he had made man on earth, and it grieved him to his heart."*

Just after God cursed the ground, evil began to multiply and dominate the heart of man. Cursing the ground did not only affect man and the land, it also affected the Lord God as well. There was no way man would prosper in his affairs when his origin was cursed. Holiness had no place in man's life, because the Lord had removed His spirit from among the people.

Genesis 6:5: *"The thoughts of his heart was only evil continually."*

The situation was getting worse, and evil dominated the entire earth.

Genesis 6:4: *"In those days, and also afterward, when the sons of God came in to the daughters of man and they bore children to them. These were the mighty men who were of old."*

The conditions were not only terrible among man on earth, but even among heavenly beings, the fallen sons of God, who went unto the daughters of man and bore children to them—the Nephilim, the offspring of the violent sons of God and the daughters of men.

All these things were the results of the curses pronounced by the Lord on the ground in order to make it hard for Adam to prosper, because he had sinned against God. Look at how many other events followed thereafter because of the disobedience of Adam. Heavenly beings are supposed to minister blessings to mankind, and after Adam was cursed, their ministration ceased and immediately some fell into sin. This is because their purpose was cut short. What God created them to do came to an end, for they were no longer working for Adam. The relationship between them and Adam in the Garden of Eden was terminated.

The very same situation can still manifest itself in your life. When your ground contains a blockage, your ministering angels lose their duties as well. These angels are supposed to work for you to soften the ground and allow you to sow as they guard and wait for harvest. The work of your hands is supposed to prosper, and you should be productive wherever God has placed you. This is because of their involvement in your life. Most people plant and do not receive anything, the reason being that their ground is blocked spiritually, and they don't become as fruitful as God intended them to be.

Jesus, the Redeemer of Our Ground

Immediately, the Lord God realized that the ground should be released and begin to function in the manner He had created it to be.

Genesis 8:20–21: *"Then Noah built an altar to the Lord and took some of every clean animal and some of every clean bird and offered burnt offerings on the altar. And when the Lord smelled the pleasing aroma, the Lord said in his heart, 'I will never again curse the ground because of man …'"*

The ground is what God thought of after He smelled Noah's sacrifice. The ground, where all things came from, had a lot of meaning before the Lord, and God spoke of them in His heart. After the flood, Noah made a burnt offering, which is the highest order of sacrifice in the Old Testament. He brought forth some of the clean animals to be offered before the Lord. This act was not as simple as one would think. These animals were not as plentiful as they had been before the flood, and they were all at a risk of becoming extinct. This, however, did not stop Noah from sacrificing to the Lord those that were clean. Noah understood that God had created everything from the beginning, and it was not in him to spare what God had given to him. That is why his particular sacrifice is called a higher-order sacrifice, for it was done with the few clean animals that were left after the flood. This became pleasing before the Lord.

Now God purposed in His heart not to ever curse the ground. But there was something missing to what God purposed in His heart to do, and that was His own sacrifice. In other words, God had to bring forth His offering that lacked blemishes as well—a clean offering, fit to seal the covenant between Him and Noah. This offering had to redeem and set the ground free from the curse He had pronounced over it. Noah had challenged God.

Luke 8:4–8: *"And when a great crowd was gathering and people from town after town came to him, he said in a parable: "A sower went out to sow his seed. And as he sowed, some fell along the path and was trampled underfoot, and the birds of the air devoured it. And some fell on the rock, and as it grew up, it withered away, because it had no moisture. And some fell among thorns, and the thorns grew up with it and choked it. And some fell into good soil and grew and yielded a hundredfold.""*

John 12:23–24; *"And Jesus answered them, 'The hour has come for the Son of Man to be glorified. Truly, truly, I say to you, unless a grain of wheat falls into the earth and dies, it remains alone; but if it dies, it bears much fruit.'"*

Jesus was now ready to go into the ground to become the seed of God—a sacrifice offered to break and abolish all curses of unproductivity. Spiritually, He came to destroy the thorns and thistles choking our growth in God's kingdom, making it hard for us to prosper and to inherit our divine assignment here on earth.

Jesus came to change the condition of the soil for you. He came to create a good, fertile ground for you, so you can plant, reap, and prosper in what you do. And, He came to claim what was kept by our ground by delivering your grain from infertility.

(Second Corinthians 5:18) *He came to reconcile us to God.*

The original thoughts God had for us should be evident and clear because He described His plans as *"plans for welfare and not for evil, to give you a future and a hope"* (Jeremiah 29:11).

Our ground is set free through Christ Jesus. Isaiah 44:3: *"For I will pour water on the thirsty land and streams on the dry ground."*

Begin to sow. Have the mind of the Lord—the mind to form things from the ground. Create new things. Begin new things, for the stage is set for you to move to higher levels. Your ground has been redeemed, and the devil has nothing to say about it. Because Noah offered his sacrifice as part of the covenant, the Lord God had to give His sacrifice as well to affirm the covenant He made with Noah. Jesus is that sacrifice from God, a pleasing aroma to all who would believe in Him.

First Kings 19:11: *"And he said, 'Go out and stand on the mount before the Lord.' And behold, the Lord passed by, and a great and strong wind tore the mountains and broke in pieces the rocks before the Lord, but the Lord was not in the wind ..."*

The wind tore the mountains and broke into pieces the rocks before the Lord, but the Lord was not in the wind. This was how God prepared for His seed, by breaking and tearing the mountains and waiting for the right time to sow His seed. He Himself was not the seed, but He is the sower.

Matthew 27:57–60: *"When it was evening, there came a rich man from Arimathea, named Joseph, who also was a disciple of Jesus. He went to Pilate and asked for the body of Jesus. Then Pilate ordered it to be given to him. And Joseph took the body and wrapped it in a clean linen shroud and laid it in his own new tomb, which he had cut in the rock …"*

Joseph went on to design the broken mountain in order to make it a conducive environment in which the seed could grow uninterrupted. Jesus was then placed in tomb the Lord God had prepared long ago by a great and strong winds when God made a way for Him in the mountains.

In the Garden of Eden when God cursed man, He cursed him together with the ground. The curse of man was associated with the ground. God cursed the ground because of man. Therefore, God sent Jesus to redeem man along with his ground.

This is one of the principles the Lord uses to reverse or conquer evil. He does it in a measure similar to the one applied in Exodus 7:8–12: *"Then the Lord said to Moses and Aaron, 'When Pharaoh says to you, "Prove yourselves by working a miracle," then you shall say to Aaron, "Take your staff and cast it down before Pharaoh, that it may become a serpent."'So Moses and Aaron went to Pharaoh and did just as the Lord commanded. Aaron cast down his staff before Pharaoh and his servants, and it became a serpent. Then Pharaoh summoned the wise men and the sorcerers, and they, the magicians of Egypt, also did the same by their secret arts. For each man cast down his staff, and they became serpents. But Aaron's staff swallowed up their staffs."*

The Lord used the same art Pharaoh's magicians used to defy the works of evil. Using the same approach God mandated, a man called Joseph, from Arimathea, who was a disciple, prepared the place for Jesus to be laid in the ground as a sacrifice of redemption. This time a word was not enough from God; because, redemption had to be done in measure and manner at which man was originally made to function- from his ground. Jesus had to be laid in the grounds because that is where productivity of man originated from, in order to make the ground productive as it was designed by God to be from the beginning.

God did not just use any other man to claim the body of Jesus. Rather, He used a man who had experienced an encounter with the salvation of the Lord—a disciple who owned a new tomb. This signifies that, before the death of Christ, people owned their lives to themselves because there was no Messiah. This led many people to be buried in their own tombs— spiritual tombs they had prepared. The rock that was cut signified the hardness and the barriers to our spiritual beings, before we see God's total radiance. Therefore, Joseph created a space for Christ to be laid in his ground. Jesus was dead when Joseph claimed Him from Pilate, and he had to bury Him in the rock he had prepared, the rock that the Lord had torn, so that Jesus could resurrect from it. He took a step of faith when he buried Jesus in his tomb, for he knew He would rise up again. This man was a disciple of Christ who never witnessed God's glory and was waiting to witness the resurrection power of God in the tomb he owned- himself. This man followed Jesus and believed in all that had been written about Him in the scroll concerning the Messiah.

This means that, before Jesus can become alive in you, what you know about Him is only in the scroll. He is a "dead" Jesus—the one you should bury in your spiritual being. How you accept Him is very important. Just like Joseph, we should use a clean linen shroud to wrap Him in. This represents renewal, sincerity, and clear thoughts, with no unclean motive. Joseph laid Jesus in his tomb; in other words, he planted Jesus in the place He expected to be. An exchange occurred. One difficult stage after laying Jesus in our "tomb" is to wait for Him to come back to life. Here, nothing is working out in your life, and you are expected to wait and believe in the Jesus who is not there, "a dead Jesus". This is when some people give up their dreams and their purpose in life. They lose faith in the resurrection of the Jesus they have accepted as their Savior. The one they laid in their hearts. They fail to patiently wait unto Him, in great expectation from the heavens to release their long awaited miracle.

Joseph just laid Jesus in the tomb and left. He did not worry about the circumstances of life; he knew that Christ was his Messiah, and He would rise.

Luke 24:1–6: *"But on the first day of the week, at early dawn, they went to the tomb, taking the spices they had prepared. And they found the stone rolled away from the tomb, but when they went in they did not find the body of the Lord Jesus. While they were perplexed about this, behold, two men stood by them in dazzling apparel. And as they were frightened and bowed their faces to the ground, the men said to them, 'Why do you seek the living among the dead? He is not here, but has risen.'"*

When you accept the Lord Jesus into your life, His power might not be revealed to you at that particular moment. There are times the glory of God is hidden and not revealed for you to see. This glory is hidden for you to take a step of faith, to provoke the power of resurrection, to begin to operate in your life. When you lay Christ into your heart, your curses might not be broken right away. That financial difficulty might not be resolved immediately, and that pain might not be healed right away. But the best thing you can do for yourself is to keep on believing, just like Joseph, that your Lord Jesus will one day resurrect in your life. In the very same heart of yours where you laid Him, He will rise, in that situation you have given up on, He will rise. Jesus rose in the tomb prepared by Joseph; therefore, prepare your place of resurrection as well. Prepare yourself for a spiritual explosion—a spiritual move of God you have never imagined exists. Create that platform in you by simply having faith in His resurrection power— something you want the world to see about the Christ in you. People will no longer associate you with the dead Jesus, but will begin to associate you with the risen Jesus. And because you allowed Him to rise in you, the chapters of the story of your life will be rewritten. You will be rewarded for waiting, and His resurrection power will be visible in your life.

Chapter 2

PRE-DESTINATION

Before Joseph, the son of Jacob, could enter Egypt, the Lord God took him through life-threatening experiences that ultimately made him who he was. His life resembled the life of a believer in the walk with his maker. In our Christian walk, there are hindrances that make it difficult for us to pursue our assignment as God's ambassadors. Understand that some people have gone through what Joseph went through, and unfortunately many did not conquer their challenges; rather, they became victims in their battles. Remember that it is not in us that we should walk to direct our steps, but know that it is the Lord's desire to see us equipped with the relevant knowledge unfolded through the life of Joseph to enable you to walk successfully with Christ Jesus.

If a person is not mindful of the following areas in life, he can easily be led to into captivity to be a slave forever. The life of Joseph was governed by divine principles to which he adhered. This made him a unique servant of the Lord. Those who did not act like Joseph were disloyal to God and to his principles, and this caused them to become victims of the snare of the enemy.

Knowing Little About Your God Is Knowing Little About Your Enemy

Genesis 37:2: *"These are the generations of Jacob. Joseph, being seventeen years old, was pasturing the flock with his brothers. He was a boy with the sons of*

Bilhah and Zilpah, his father's wives. And Joseph brought a bad report of them to their father."

A seventeen-year-old boy is very young and has very little knowledge of life experiences and the manner in which he should conduct himself. At this young age, Joseph did not see his family members as a threat to what God had destined for him. His mind told him that all was well, and he was safer when he revealed his purpose to his brothers.

Our association with others when we begin our journey with the Lord is very crucial: that is, the stage when we are young in our walk with Christ. When a person accepts the Lord as his personal Savior, sometimes the first people to try to discredit him are the people closest to him. These are the people who know that person's upbringing. The problem begins when God begins to speak to you. Now your acts have changed, your talk is different, and the devil has realized that he has lost you, and you are no longer his. You have begun to understand who you are from the scripture. You are no longer blind, but now you see, and you have confessed Jesus as your personal Savior. He has become your Lord, and you are His servant. Christ has become your life, and everything you have revolves around Him. Seeing this, the devil begins to gather adversaries, and the quickest people for him to use are the people closest to you.

Mathew 10:34–36: *"Do not think that I have come to bring peace to the earth. I have not come to bring peace, but a sword. For I have come to set a man against his father, and a daughter against her mother, and a daughter-in-law against her mother-in-law. And a person's enemies will be those of his own household."*

When you decide to pursue the way of the Lord, you become young in the ways of the Lord. Members of your family may raise opposition. Joseph's adversaries came from his own household. Sometimes, one member from a family will choose to follow Christ, but others will choose a different route. When you are surrounded by negative, condemning people, especially if they happen to be members of your family, know that it is scriptural and the matter is under God's control.

People who know little about their God will not understand what the Lord is doing and will, in turn retaliate. This is where the devil takes advantage and totally destroys the plan of God for your life. Our God is a wise God, and what we should always learn from Him is how He operates. It is all written in His word. The more we learn about God, the more God reveals the schemes of the devil in our lives. The more you search the scriptures, the more your fears fade away; and the more we talk to Him, the more we are filled with His nature.

There are many ways to know the Lord, and one of the most powerful ways besides His word is to listen to the testimonies of His people. A testimony is a powerful weapon to assist believers in what the Lord has done for His people.

John 4:28–30: *"So the woman left her water jar and went away into town and said to the people, 'Come, see a man who told me all that I ever did. Can this be the Christ?' They went out of the town and were coming to him."*

Just imagine what could have happened if the same woman had kept quiet and said absolutely nothing to the people. Then the villagers could have missed an encounter with Christ. Jesus did not send this woman. In her excitement, the woman testified. The woman did not call her family only, but she called everyone. Some people in the town that day just stood and ignored her call. They said to themselves, "Well! We thought as much. This is the very same woman again. Who has she met this time around?" And this is how they missed their encounter with Jesus. A testimony carries a magnetic force that attracts others to their faith in the Lord.

It does not matter who gives a testimony. It does not matter how many times a person has failed in life. In fact, God works more in the lives of the people who have experienced series of failures. Testimonies don't go hand in hand with looks and appearances. They are the works of the Lord that, by grace, can fall on anyone. Anybody can testify.

John 1:19–27: *"And this is the testimony of John, when the Jews sent priests and Levites from Jerusalem to ask him, 'Who are you?' He confessed, and did not deny, but confessed, 'I am not the Christ.' And they asked him, 'What then?*

Are you Elijah?' He said, 'I am not.' 'Are you the Prophet?' And he answered, 'No.' so they said to him, 'Who are you? We need to give an answer to those who sent us. What do you say about yourself?' He said, 'I am the voice of one crying out in the wilderness, "Make straight the way of the Lord," as the prophet Isaiah said.' (Now they had been sent from the Pharisees.) They asked him, 'Then why are you baptizing, if you are neither the Christ, nor Elijah, nor the Prophet?' John answered them, 'I baptize with water, but among you stands one you do not know, even he who comes after me, the strap of whose sandal I am not worthy to untie.'"

The testimony of John the Baptist has shaken the entire world from the time he testified about Christ till today. His testimony has resolved many questions about baptism. John testified about Jesus, because he knew his God. He also knew the works and the heart of the Pharisees, for God spoke about them from His word. His testimony regarding Christ became an encouraging tool to the church of God. John 1:32–34: *"And John bore witness: 'I saw the Spirit descend from heaven like a dove, and it remained on him. I myself did not know him, but he who sent me to baptize with water said to me, "He on whom you see the Spirit descend and remain, this is he who baptizes with the Holy Spirit. And I have seen and have borne witness that this is the Son of God."'"*

John did not know who Jesus was, but the Lord God spoke to him of how Jesus would appear. John had to bear this testimony even if he himself did not know who Jesus was. He had to believe in the voice of the one who told him about the coming of Christ and how the Holy Spirit would act when he had an encounter with Jesus.

Jesus one day said to Thomas: *"Blessed are those who have not seen and yet have believed"* (John 20:29).

John the Baptist had a positive attitude toward what he heard about Jesus. He had also personally discovered information from the scroll concerning the coming of the Messiah. John the Baptist gave testimony about Him who is greater and what the voice of the Lord ministered to him about. He did not know Jesus, but he spoke like somebody who had already seen Him. And after he saw Him, he bore witness to Him, the Son of the living God

As a believer, you should testify about what the Lord has done for you, and you should appreciate the works of God in other people's lives. The devil hates it when you testify about Christ, because he does not want people to know what God does for them.

Maybe the Lord is beginning to show you the steps you should take, just as He did with Joseph in his earlier years, and you are excited about it. Do not stop to talk about Him. Testify to his goodness from His word and what He is doing in your life. Do not allow circumstances of life to rob you of your testimony of the Lord. The devil prevents believers from testifying, and if they testify, he prevents others from believing their testimony.

Just believe that one day you will see Jesus working in your life. Just as Paul saw Him on the road to Damascus, you will be a witness. He became a witness to what others have testified about.

Second Chronicles 20:10–11: *"And now behold, the men of Ammon and Moab and Mount Seir, whom you would not let Israel invade when they came from the land of Egypt, and whom they avoided and did not destroy—behold, they reward us by coming to drive us out of your possession, which you have given us to inherit."*

Knowing little about your God is knowing little about your enemies.

The Lord is the one who reveals the plans of the enemies to us. How then can He reveal anything to you when you don't know Him?

Jehoshaphat knew that God would not allow the Israelites to invade the men of Ammon and Moab and Mount Seir when they came from the land of Egypt. Knowing their God, they followed His direction and did not invade these lands, based on what the Lord had commanded. Because God instructed the Israelites that they should not invade the men of Ammon and they obeyed, He also revealed the schemes of the men of Ammon toward Jehoshaphat, warning him of the attack they were planning against

Israel. These were the very same nations God spared; this was returning good with evil.

If the children of Israel could have ignored the words of the Lord to spare the men of Moab, God could have ignored the plots of these nations made against them. But now, Jehoshaphat knew the Lord, and he confidently ran to Him to remind Him of the obedience they had once submitted to with regard to what the Lord had commanded of them concerning the men of Moab. The nations that had their own lands wanted to possess the land of the Israelites. The Lord did not allow that to happen, especially after sparing these same nations.

Second Chronicles 20:15: *"Thus says the Lord to you, 'Do not be afraid and do not be dismayed at this great horde, for the battle is not yours but God's.'"* Jehoshaphat was just minding his business when two men came to tell him about what the Ammonites were planning against Israel. It was not in Jehoshaphat to know of these ambushes against him, but God made it a point to reveal this plot when he was least expecting it. This is what the Lord God does for the people who know what He can do for them. These men who came to Jehoshaphat were sent by the Lord simply because Jehoshaphat was blameless and did whatever it took to seek the Lord first in everything he did for his kingdom.

Second Chronicles 20:3: *"Then Jehoshaphat was afraid and set his face to seek the Lord, and proclaimed a fast throughout all Judah."*

In our walk with the Lord we are surrounded by a great horde … a great multitude that comes against us even when we have done good to them. They reward us with evil. David said in Psalm 109:2–5: *"For wicked and deceitful mouths are opened against me, speaking against me with lying tongues. They encircle me with words of hate, and attack me without cause. In return for my love they accuse me, but I give myself to prayer. So they reward me evil for good, and hatred for my love."*

Do you think that, because you are doing good to people, serving them and assisting them in times of their need, they will in return do good to you? That's not always the case, but know that such evil awaits people who do good to others, and God will never forsake those who know who He is and what He can do for those who seek Him.

When You Are God's Beloved

Genesis 37:3: *"Now Israel loved Joseph more than any other of his sons, because he was the son of his old age."*

One major thing that makes the devil hate you so much is the love that God has toward you.

When Joseph was out with his brothers, he brought a bad report of them to their father (Genesis 37:2). This means that Joseph was a loyal, trustworthy person who always brought about his affairs to his father, especially when he was away with his brothers from their father's presence.

One of our weaknesses as Christians is the behavior we portray when we are far away from other Christians. We tend to behave differently, and this creates a serious problem in our spiritual walk with the Lord. When the Lord was about to hand over the land of promise to the Israelites, Moses took twelve men, *"one man from each tribe. And they turned and went up into the hill country, and came to the Valley of Eshcol and spied it out. And they took in their hands some of the fruit of the land and brought it down to us, and brought us word again and said, 'It is a good land that the Lord our God is giving us.' Yet you would not go up, but rebelled against the command of the Lord your God. And you murmured in your tents and said, 'Because the Lord hated us he has brought us out of the land of Egypt, to give us into the hand of the Amorites, to destroy us'"*(Deuteronomy 1:23–27).

Deuteronomy 1:34–36: *"And the Lord heard your words and was angered, and he swore, 'Not one of these men of this evil generation shall see the good land that I swore to give to your fathers, except Caleb the son of Jephunneh.'"*

The Hebrew origin of the name *Caleb* refers to faith, devotion, and whole heartedness. Because of this meaning of Caleb, it is clear why God spoke well of him. God was not pleased with other men who went to spy out the land. These men brought in some of the fruits of the land as evidence of what the land produced, and they brought in a good report about the land and its products. Their report was convincing, because it showed that they believed that God had given them good land where they would find plenty to eat. But, secretly, these men did not trust in the Lord, and they murmured and spoke evil against the very same land they had given a good report about. This angered the Lord (Deuteronomy 1:26–27). Unlike Caleb, these men lacked faith, and their actions were contrary to what they said. Hebrews 11:6: *"And without faith it is impossible to please him [God]."*

How do you personally respond to the ways of the Lord? What report are you secretly giving about the Lord? Are you publicly praising something that the Lord will use to elevate you, but in your secret corners doubting the very works of the Lord in your life?

The name Caleb carries attributes that will give you solutions that can help you to possess your land of promise. Caleb, meaning devotion, simply means to apply oneself to something with seriousness. Caleb did not just go to spy out the land because he was sent; he was devoted to what he did. He was committed to please God, and he worked earnestly with dedication to see himself giving a good report, to Him who sent him. He knew how important the land was to Him and His people.

The Lord has also called us to assemblies called churches to devote ourselves to Him and by dedicating our lives to back to Him. Whatever report we give in our secret places should reflect what we have publicly proclaimed the Lord will do for us. Caleb worked wholeheartedly for the Lord; he understood that the land he was sent to was a promised land many desired to enter but could not.

Joseph and Caleb had something in common; that is, they brought a pleasing report to the one who sent them. All God's children are sent into the circular world to represent Christ in speech, actions, and lifestyle. Also, these men, Caleb and Joseph, were surrounded by people who lacked interest in the ways of the Lord …people who were good at praising the works of God in public, but within lacked a single spark to ignite their belief. When you find yourself among such people, know that God has strategically placed you in their midst to sharpen your vision by focusing more on His goodness rather than on what others say.

Murmuring against the Lord sometimes is viewed as a small thing among believers, but in fact most people who murmured in the Bible were viewed by the Lord as evil. They failed to satisfy the Lord, and hence never reached their destination (1 Corinthians 10:9–10).

Luke 5:29–32: *"And Levi made him a great feast in his house, and there was a huge company of tax collectors and other reclining at table with them. And the Pharisees and their scribes grumbled at his disciples saying, 'Why do you eat and drink with tax collectors and sinners?' And Jesus answered them, 'Those who are well have no need of a physician, but those who are sick. I have not come to call the righteous but sinners to repentance.'"*

Already the Pharisees and their scribes had missed their salvation, because they failed to acknowledge the coming of Messiah into their lives, and grumbling was a sign of their dissatisfaction. So Jesus saw them as "righteous" and plainly said to them He had not come for the righteous, but rather had come for those who sought salvation. The Pharisees and their scribes missed their salvation, because they failed to repent. They failed to accommodate Him who saves the lost even as they themselves were lost.

Luke 15:1–2: *"Now the tax collectors and sinner were all drawing near to hear him. And the Pharisees and the scribes grumbled, saying, 'This man receives sinners and eats with them.'"*

And Jesus said, *"Just so, I tell you, there will be more joy in heaven over one sinner who repents than over ninety-nine righteous persons who need no repentance"* (Luke 15:7).

Again, who was grumbling? The Pharisees, over the same matter: repentance. This time Jesus told them about the joy that is experienced by the heavens over a sinner who repents. Jesus repeated the same statement He made when He said, *"I have not come to call the righteous but sinners to repentance"* (Luke 5:32). The Pharisees failed to see the love Jesus had for the lost, and they in return missed the love God had prepared for them.

As Joseph and Caleb did, it is possible to see only the good things in situations. As a believer, what you see and how you see it are very important. Christians have supernatural eyes of faith, and they can dictate situations to their favor. You are God's beloved. See yourself through His word, and you shall find His promises of love for you. Murmuring and complaining can be substituted by faith, devotion, and dedication to God's works.

Psalm 51:17: *"The sacrifices of God are a broken spirit; a broken and contrite heart, O God, you will not despise."*

At a tender age, Joseph demonstrated the trust he had for his father, Jacob. He confided in him, and he was not influenced by what his brothers were doing. This gave him a good reputation before his father. Similarly, God is pleased when broken and contrite hearts are offered to Him when we encounter setbacks in lives. Joseph gave a bad report of his brothers, and we should also continually give of our bad report; in other words, we must confess our sins before the Lord, for by so doing we will be destroying the chains of sin in our lives, and His love for us will abound forever.

Colossians 1:12: *"Giving thanks to the father, who has qualified you to share in the inheritance of the saints in light."*

When you report to God your weaknesses and your fears, He will in return qualify you to share in His inheritance; whatever bad report you tell of yourself before Him will work to your favor, and the Lord will speak well of you. He will show you His love, and He will qualify you above the rest.

Carrying Something Others Are Not Carrying

Genesis 37:7–11 *"'Behold, we were binding sheaves in the field, and behold, my sheaf arose and stood upright. And behold, your sheaves gathered around it and bowed down to my sheaf.' His brothers said to him, 'Are you indeed to reign over us? Or are you indeed to rule over us?' So they hated him even more for his dreams and for his words. Then he dreamed another dream and told it to his brothers and said, 'Behold, I have dreamed another dream. Behold, the sun, the moon, and the eleven stars were bowing down to me.' But when he told it to his father and to his brothers, his father rebuked him and said to him, 'What is this dream that you have dreamed? Shall I and your mother and your brothers indeed come and bow ourselves to the ground before you?' And his brothers were jealous of him, but his father kept the saying in mind."*

His father rebuked him. Jacob did not understand Joseph's two dreams. He rebuked his son for such dreams of greatness.

When God introduced Himself, He said; *"I am the God of Abraham, the God of Isaac, the God of Jacob"* (Matthew 22:32). To each one of them he was God. He did not say, "I am the God of Abraham, Isaac, and Jacob." God did not speak about these men collectively. He said, *"I am the God of Abraham, the God of Isaac."* This means that the God that Abraham and Isaac knew was the same God Jacob knew, but revealed Himself differently to each one of them. Jacob could see God's hand in the lives of Abraham and Isaac, and how He related with each one of them, but he would not understand their experiences to God as he himself knew and experienced God in his life. One would think that, because God called Himself by the name "God of Jacob", Jacob would have had a revelation from Him of the life of Joseph, his great son, but that was not the case, for God kept the life of Joseph from him. Jacob did not have a single thought that Joseph would be greater than he. He loved Joseph, but not to the extent of imagining him to be greater than himself. "How would that be?" he thought to himself. Even if God called himself by the name of his servant, Jacob, He still hid one important aspect of his life, and that was the greatness of Joseph. This was kept from him, because he could have immediately embraced the two dreams of Joseph, and right away make preparation for his greatness in a way that God was not intending, and later claiming the glory. God wanted to raise Joseph into greatness alone without anybody's assistance. If the people you expect to embrace your dreams are also part of the dream, then how will they unfold it for you?

As a person seeking solutions for your destiny, you must realize that the one and only person who has all the steps to your greatness is God Himself. Do not get crossed when you want a particular matter in your life to be resolved through the man of God and it is not, for he himself does not know everything, since all things are revealed by the Lord… This is where most of us fail; we fail to understand that our spiritual parents are also hearing from God, and God may not reveal your dreams to them. Now this is where most people begin to lose hope. They assume that God does not have great plans for them, especially when their spiritual parent can't unfold what they are going through. Do not allow yourself to have that mentality; rather, convince yourself that all your steps are ordered by God Himself, and at a heavenly right time, your matter will be resolved. God has kept secret the one who will bring you the keys to your elevation—that one thing you have always wanted. Your solutions are known only to Him.

This matter caused confusion between Joseph and Jacob, his father. Joseph did not know how he would become great, and Jacob did not know that Joseph would become great. God has never revealed to a person all the steps he should take in life in order to attain his or her destination. He does this so that we consistently and diligently seek Him.

Joseph's First Dream

Joseph had two dreams of greatness. The first one is the upright dream. An upright position is a vertical and erect posture. In biblical terms, you are upright when you strictly adhere to God's word and are righteous.

This dream was a dream about upright sheaves. First we should understand that you cannot bind sheaves before you harvest, and you can't harvest unless you first water the plants; therefore, it all begins by sowing the right seed.

What God meant from this dream to Joseph was, if a person become upright, and his live is pleasing before Him, he will be stronger and attractive compared to other people. Others will envy his production. Joseph's life had to be upright in order for him to receive what the Lord had promised him. Joseph had to sow only righteousness in order for God to sustain him and keep all his steps.

You must walk upright before the Lord if you want God to fulfill His promises to you. God's principles require each and every person to live right with Him and others, and to strictly adhere to His commands, keeping all biblical principles diligently.

To Joshua the Lord said, *"This book of the law shall not depart from your mouth, but you shall meditate on it day and night, so that you may be careful to do according to all that is written in it"* (Joshua 1:8).

Meditation is one attribute you can use to water the words God has spoken from His book. It acts as a fertilizer, making your seeds grow faster. And you can harvest more just by meditation.

Meditating on God's word is a doorway to revelations from His word that will lead you to your next higher step toward your goal. It gives access to supernatural victories where solutions are attained to silence all voices announcing failure to your destination. Irresolvable matters are resolved through meditation. When God says you should meditate on the Book of Life, He wants you to meet your needs through the manner in which you think of Him. He wants to give you solutions to your problems in a manner to which you alone will have the access code. To what you understand. Meditation on God's words ushers holiness; it aligns righteousness and nourishes spirituality by breaking bonds and curses that limit and hinder your elevation. It is important, because you must first visualize yourself blessed before others pronounce blessings upon you. You should see yourself elevated by destroying the chains of doubt before others think of elevating you. When your mind comes into contact with God's word, you contact success.

Joshua 1:8: *"For then you will make your way prosperous and then you will have good success."*

God commanded Joshua to succeed and be prosperous. He commanded him to gain access to his greatness, and that was through the book of law;

in other words, God was saying to Joshua, "I command you to be blessed, to prosper, and to succeed in everything you do."

Joshua 1:9: *"Have I not commanded you? Be strong and courageous. Do not be frightened, and do not be dismayed, for the Lord your God is with you wherever you go."*

What are the commands in this passage? Being strong and being courageous. Are these commands? Yes they are! Being strong is a command. And not being frightened or dismayed is also a command from the Lord. These are the commands that were given to Joshua. The name *Joshua* means "a deliverer." These were the same attributes that Joseph possessed through righteous living. Are you a deliverer? Then the world is waiting for you, and the Lord is commanding you to be strong and courageous when opposition rises against you.

Joseph's Second Dream

Joseph's second dream was a dream of luminosity. It speaks in general about the measure of brightness that Joseph carried. In astronomy, luminosity is said to be the measure of the total amount of energy emitted by a star, and the power of the output of the sun. Thus, out of the brightness of light there is power and energy.

An observer on earth perceives the brightness of the sun, the moon, and the stars as visible wavelengths. In other words, we can describe the amount of emission or the brightness of light from luminous objects. The sun and the moon emit more light than a star. Joseph's dream was saying that Joseph will emit a greater light than all earthly objects that emit light in the universe, to an extent that other sources of light will not be recognized at His presence. This was a plain insult to Joseph's parents and brothers, because to them, a greater light was the sun, which was suppose to be Jacob and not Joseph.

Genesis 1:16: *"And God made the great lights—the greater light to rule the day and the lesser light to rule the night—and the stars."*

All these lights that God made were not greater than God. God also made another greater light in Joseph's life, a greater light other lights would bow down to.

Isaiah 60:19: *"The sun shall be no more your light by day, nor for brightness shall the moon give you light; but the Lord will be your everlasting light, and your God will be your glory."*

The light in Joseph's life was the Lord Himself! Joseph was carrying the glory of the Lord, the light greater than all the light on earth. With such an amount of brightness, Joseph needed to do only one thing, and that was to preserve the Lord's glory.

The enemy knows when an individual carries this light, and in situations like this, the Lord puts him on board to use him to elevate you. He becomes like a scaffold used to erect a very high building. In his attempt to quench God's glory in you, he's indirectly laying a brick. Every brick he thought he used to stone you with has been put in place, and a mansion has been erected. Understand the role of the enemy in your life; if he is near, a godly character can come forth; as a defense.

Bacteria are said to cause many diseases, such as respiratory infections, but generally they play a major role in breaking down organic molecules into their compounds. They recycle nature. Biologists claim that, without bacteria, life would cease to exist. Carbon, nitrogen, and phosphorus are essential organic substances that are broken down from waste substances by bacteria. Without these microorganisms, nitrogen fixation in agriculture would not take place. Bacteria is also used in cheese production, as well as in the production of many foods and beverages. Even if some bacteria are pathogens, a large amount of them are essential. Joseph's brothers were like bacteria to him. They opened a doorway to his success. Begin to see life's disappointments like that. Your hindrances are like bacteria that are essential for your ability to create "cheese" in this lifetime. Do not allow the glory of the Lord to be snatched from you by evil men. Protect that vision the Lord has given to you, and allow God's glory to emit the greatest light the enemy cannot stand against.

Acts 6:8–9: *"And Stephen, full of grace and power, was doing great wonders and signs among the people. Then some of those who belonged to the synagogue of the Freedmen (as it was called), and of the Cyrenians, and of the Alexandrians, and of those from Cilicia and Asia, rose up and disputed with Stephen."*

Expect dispute if you know that you are carrying a greater light than others are carrying. If you know that your destiny is great, anticipate opposition. You can't run, for you are the light, and wherever you go, you will be visible. If the glory and the power of the Lord are found in an individual, then check his surroundings. You will hear voices that want to suppress and cover the glory.

Acts 5:38–39: *"So in the present case I tell you, keep away from these men and let them alone, for if this plan or this undertaking is of man it will fail, but if it is of God, you will not be able to overthrow them. You might even be found opposing God!' So they took their advice."*

Advise your opposition to leave you alone, for they are opposing God not you. They are opposing the greater light … the one that cannot be quenched! Men and women who are called into greatness by God cannot be overthrown. They are children of the light, for they carry God. It is not they who work in their lives, but it is God, ushering them to their destiny. They are spirit filled, and the works of evil cannot prevail against them, for their steps are ever before the Lord, their maker. Do not be frightened by the sudden terror, for the Lord is your refuge.

Esther 7:9–10: *"Then Harbona, one of the eunuchs in attendance on the king said, 'Moreover, the gallows that Haman has prepared for Mordecai, whose word saved the king, is standing at Haman's house, fifty cubits high.' And the king said, 'Hang him on that.' So they hanged Haman on the gallows that he had prepared for Mordecai. Then the wrath of the king abated."*

Haman wanted to end the life of the child of light. He built a fifty-cubit-tall gallows on which to hang Mordecai. News rose of the kindness that Mordecai had once shown the king. It was Haman, the high official in King Xerxes" kingdom who was hanged on the same gallows that he had prepared for Mordecai. God is sending confusion into the opposition's camp. A disagreement is taking place; those who were favored will lose their favor before their king, and your name will be mentioned for elevation.

When you are destined for greatness, every evil plot is to your advantage. The Lord will remember the kindness you once did for others, and what was forgotten about you will be revealed, and the enemy will fall on the very same snare that he laid for you. God is always by your side no matter the kind of plot the enemy has laid against you and He will see you over your next greatest hurdle towards your destiny.

You Are a Messenger of the Word

Genesis 37:14: *"So he said to him, 'Go now, see if it is well with your brothers and with the stock and bring me word.' So he sent from the valley of Hebron, and he came to Schechem."*

Schechem was said to be one of the busiest locations in Israel. It was home to most important crossroads to central Israel. The road to Schechem that Joseph was sent on forced him to pass through the valley of Hebron, between two mountains. Valleys signify a low or difficult period encountered in a person's walk with the Lord. In a valley, believers go through hard times coupled with a lot of suffering. This is a stage in which destiny is blurred and the road of salvation becomes questionable to many concerning their lives. Joseph had to go through that valley when he was sent by Jacob to look for his brothers.

Valleys and mountains are often used by the Lord to seek those who would say, *"For still the vision awaits its appointed time; it hastens to the end—it will not lie. If it seems slow, wait for it; it will surely come; it will not delay"* (Habakkuk 2:3). Situations can interfere with your steps when you don't interfere with them. It is only when you allow them space on your path that they will prevent you from moving. When doubt storms your heart, and your walk seems faint, you will need to hear only that one voice telling you that, "God's promises will not lie, the vision He gave you concerning your destiny awaits its appointed time." When your vision dies, so will your inner drive. When you no longer see the vision you used to see and you cannot perform the things you used to perform concerning your future, know that your journey has been covered by the enemy. Visions are there to simply let you know that God has granted you victory over your doubts. It is one thing to doubt yourself, and it is another to doubt God, for God is the provider of all good things, and the dreams you are having to provide for the needs of others are from Him. And for all that you want to gain in life, God has granted you the platform here on earth; everything is set for you.

Jacob sent Joseph along that valley to seek his brothers and their flocks. The difficulties Joseph experienced on his journey represent the life difficulties a believer encounters on his journey to attain his goals. That path to Schechem had mountains, a valley, and crossroads. It was a busy location. A mountain, a valley, and crossroads have no external personal influences on a person toward his or her goals in life. What does this mean? It means that they are not there to hinder you or to prevent you from keeping on, for they are not in motion to stand before you. What makes people weak and weary in their pursuit of their destiny is their own personal intake of knowledge, insight, and resources. When you travel without thorough preparation, you are bound to get weary. A road athlete inspects his route by a car first before going into serious training on the road by foot. Some athletes interview those who have competed on that very road in order to know how they should outline their preparations. This is how we should be in our preparations towards our walk with Christ. The Lord wrote to us in His word and told us how we should walk in our journey with Him, because He does not want us to be weary on the road; Jesus said, *"I am the way"* (John 14:6).

The emphasis is on Jacobs" words when he sent Joseph he said to him: *"Go now …"* (Genesis 37:14). The moment the devil hears these words, which release you into greatness; he begins to raise challenges around your life and begins to frighten you with mountains and valleys. When God speaks a word to release you to achieve your goals, the devil will raise doubts in your mind and cause you to worry about how you will crossover and succeed at that project you have long wanted to do. Remember, mountains and valleys don't move; they cannot hinder your destiny. Ignore them and focus on your goals. Fill your mind with enough words of hope from the Lord; and by so doing, you will not entertain the devil's schemes to discourage you. People who entertain their problems are problems themselves. Time in the kingdom of God is of essential importance. If the Lord commands you to *"Go now ..."* and open that business, that is the appointed time. Messengers wait to perform the word that comes out of the mouth of their king. Children of the most high should understand that evangelism is the heartbeat of the Lord. God is sending each believer one way or another to his brothers and to the entire flock. Evangelism cannot succeed only by ministry or preaching alone; God also uses other channels as well—sports, business, academia, and hospitality—to equip those who will be trustworthy to share His kingdom with others in those areas.

Acts 6:1–4: *"Now in these days when the disciples were increasing in number, a complaint by the Hellenists arose against the Hebrews because their widows were being neglected in the daily distribution. And the twelve summoned the full number of the disciples and said, 'It is not right that we should give up preaching the word of God to serve tables. Therefore, brothers, pick out from among you seven men of good repute, full of the Spirit and wisdom, whom we will appoint to this duty. But we will devote ourselves to prayer and to the ministry of the word.'"*

The apostles divided themselves; some preached and some served tables. This means that God chose some to preach and others to prepare food. When God places you in other avenues besides preaching, you are still sent to minister His word wherever He has placed you. When Joseph was sent to his brothers by his father, he said he should "see" if all was well with his brothers (Genesis 37:14). Sometimes it is hard for a person to just "see" or look down at circumstances that are intended to pull him or her down. Disputes in life can engage us in physical warfare against our persecutors instead of allowing us to "see" or look upon the crises as we devote ourselves in prayer.

Acts 7:54: *"Now when they heard these things they were enraged, and they ground their teeth at him. But he, full of the Holy Spirit, gazed into heaven and saw the glory of God and Jesus standing at the right hand of God. And he said, 'Behold, I see the heavens opened, and the son of man standing at the right hand of God.' But they cried out with a loud voice and stopped their ears and rushed together at him. Then they cast him out of the city and stoned him. And the witnesses laid down their garments at the feet of a young man named Saul."*

The man called Saul, spoken of in this passage, is the very same apostle Paul, who later became the mighty man of the gospel. He was in the midst of those who stoned Stephen. An interest is drawn to Stephen's garment that was laid at Saul's feet by those who witnessed what happened. The question is, did they witness what Stephen said about seeing Christ at the right-hand side of God, or did they witness the stoning only? In the midst of confusion and pain, what do you choose to see? Do you choose to see the pain or the gain? The garment that was laid at the feet of Saul was a divine arrangement symbolizing that he should continue where Stephen left off. In the midst of confusion and pain, somebody saw his divine assignment. Somebody received a calling from the Lord. What do you chose to see? Do you choose to see the heavens shout for you? You see, the heavens are always open whether you are the person stoned at or the person assigned to do the stoning? Some people believe that, whenever heaven is open, all things should be well and good, and whenever heaven is closed, all things should be tough and bad. Well this is not the principle that describes the heavens. The heavens are always open to someone, so choose what you want to see around you. Do you choose to see the stoning or the impartation God offers to you through the garments of His vessels? Or do you choose to see the father and the son you should witness about?

God chose to impart a message to Saul through the garment worn by Stephen in the midst of violence. To Saul there was no implication, but God knew his ministry was been given birth to. If Stephen could have fought his way out and thrown back stones as well, the hand of God would not be evident in his life, and Saul could have missed the impartation throughout his life. This shows that messengers of the word should not fight their own battles, for in that battle, the will of God is been manifested. When disaster struck Stephen's life, he did only one thing—he gazed into heaven. His eyes were not on his persecutors; rather, he looked intently with great interest at the one who had sent him. Stephen allowed God to take care of his surroundings. He did not mention a single name of anybody he was familiar with; that was not important to him, because his God was present. One way to determine if God is present is to monitor your surroundings. When He appears, all evil appears and manifest. The demons that were holding your keys to life will break loose, for darkness has no communion with light. In your life, when evil manifests around you, know and understand that God, along with the son and the spirit, is present; therefore, make a decision to believe the situation you want to see in your life.

Bringing back the word

A report and the word of God are different from one another, and their objectives are not the same. A report gives a messenger liberty to give a feedback based on his or her experiences and on what he or she knows and understands, but delivering God's word has nothing to do with the messenger. When you are sent with God's word, it is the message that dominates and not the messenger. Messengers of a report carry a report, whereas messengers of God's word are carried by the word. The word becomes the totality of their being, because they do everything from it. A messenger of God's word is commanded on what to do, how to do it, and when and where it should be proclaimed. The word he is sent with does not change; it is the same when he goes and when he returns it back to his master. Messengers of the word speak only what they are commanded to speak, and they perform their duties on what the word says. They witness the manifestation of the word, its power, and its effect on those who have an encounter with it. Messengers of God's word have nothing else to proclaim besides the word they are sent with. These messengers ultimately become that word themselves.

Word against Words

Ezekiel 2:1–5: *"And he said to me, 'Son of man, stand on your feet and I will speak with you.' And as he spoke to me, the Spirit entered into me and set me on my feet, and I heard him speaking to me. And he said to me, 'Son of man, I send you to the people of Israel, to nations of rebels, who have transgressed against me. They and their fathers have transgressed against me to this very day.*

The descendants also are impudent and stubborn: I send you to them, and you shall say to them, "Thus says the Lord God." And whether they hear or refuse to hear (for they are a rebellious house) they will know that a prophet has been among them. And you, son of man, be not afraid of them, nor be afraid of their words, though briers and thorns are with you and you sit on scorpions. Be not afraid of their words, nor be dismayed of their looks, for they are a rebellious house. And you shall speak my words to them, whether they hear or refuse to hear, for they are a rebellious house."'

When God sent Ezekiel to the rebels of Israel, He said something most messengers don't want to hear, especially from God. He said that briers, thorns, and scorpion would be with them where He commanded them to go. God did not want to hide from Ezekiel what he would have to go through as a messenger of the word; He made it part of the message. Scorpions and thorns exist in the journey with the Lord; they are a reality. And if you are not well rooted in the word, they can easily prevent you from taking your next step of faith. God was making a statement to Ezekiel that these thorns couldn't be avoided. They are a significant tool God uses to assist you in accomplishing your assignment toward your mission and purpose. Those who endure become privileged, and they are no longer called messengers, but sons of God.

Ezekiel was a kind of messenger who would do anything for the Lord. He accepted that he must pass through the obstacles God told him about. God revealed to Ezekiel the pains he would suffer, because he trusted how He would deliver him from them. When God trusts in a person, He is actually trusting in what His potential can do in that person's life. Therefore, whenever you rise, God sees His potential enabling you to rise. Whatever your success, God sees Himself succeeding through you. What you acquire is acquired by God, and when you rejoice in the Lord midst of pain, the Lord is glorified and grants you healing, because whatever you go through, He suffers the same. Most people refuse to go where there are scorpions and thorns, because they are afraid of pain, but they fail to understand that pain is a shadow of everyman, and it is better to experience pain with the Lord than to go through it alone, for God is the comforter of the brokenhearted. Who else knows how to comfort besides the comforter? God sent Ezekiel through undesirable paths. His life was in danger for proclaiming God's word. His ministry was to rebuke and to reconcile the rebellious house of Jerusalem to God, and if they refused to obey, he was mandated to pronounce judgment and send them into exile. God knew very well the kind of people He was sending Ezekiel to, and in the process he had to build Ezekiel's character to be equal to the task he had set him to, by instilling in him courage and boldness to face them.

Before God sent Ezekiel to the rebellious nation, Ezekiel was very fearful and weak. He fell to the ground, but God released His spirit to raise him up and to make him stand on his feet so his assignment could begin. It is only the word that comes out of God's mouth that will raise you up onto your feet so you can take your next step. When God spoke, His spirit entered the weak flesh of Ezekiel. The same spirit is present today for those who don't know what to do and how to do it. God is speaking into your life today, and your destiny is unfolding through God's word. When Ezekiel stood, it was no longer he who functioned; it was God's spirit in him. And so shall be the case with your life. It will no longer be you who functions; it will be God's spirit. Therefore, do not limit God's spirit. Whatever vision the spirit places in your mind, it is possible. This is what made Ezekiel fearless and able to confront the nation of Israel alone. God never sends a messenger empty handed; He equips His messengers with power and boldness to overcome scorpions and to uproot thorns and briers that are planted on their way. Only the word will raise you to that God-given mandate just as it raised Ezekiel. God's spirit cannot fail to live in you. God is waiting for anyone to come out who desires to make an impact upon his generation. With the spirit, there is no weakness, and fear has no opportunity to capture your dreams. Therefore, rise and take that great step, for the spirit of God lives in you.

The nation of Israel rejected the very word Ezekiel was sent to them about. They refused to hear him, just as God had predicted. When what you are sent for refuses to manifest, and the doors you are supposed to enter through refuse to be open, there is only one thing remaining for you to do, and that is to pronounce judgment on your destiny holders, those situations that do not want to let go and allow your breakthrough.

When God releases you to your future, whatever opposes you and refuses to submit to your coming is silenced by judgment. God can captivate the opposition and send it into exile so you can acquire your freedom and work toward your destiny. The spirit of God enabled Ezekiel to overcome the evil words that came out of the mouths of people. These people disqualified and limited the magnitude of God's potential through Ezekiel. Israel believed that God's word was empty and without meaning, but despite that, Ezekiel proclaimed the word of the Lord even if they refused to hear him. The word of God is alive, and when you remain silent without pronouncing it, your environment will not know that God's spirit was once present. God told Ezekiel that, after Ezekiel left the nation, the people would know that a prophet had been among them.

If you don't attend to the cords that are holding your miracle, how will they know that you are carrying God's power without putting it to use? When you see result, you also become confident as a messenger. You know that you have spoken continually, and you know you have succeeded, this is a key. That is: speak it anyway. One would ask, then, if God knew that these people would not hear, why did He not act on their rebellion immediately instead of sending Ezekiel? Whose words should prevail? God's word or their words? The word of God is the same whether He sends a messenger or He speaks to the people Himself. His word does not change, and its effect is the same; therefore, every situation should bow to the voice that comes out of the mouth of a messenger one way or another. Messengers should convince themselves that every word of the Lord that comes out their mouths represents God Himself, and whatever they speak, God is the one speaking it Himself.

Isaiah 55:11: *"So shall my word be that goes out from my mouth; it shall not return to me empty, but it shall accomplish that which I purpose, and shall succeed in the thing for which I sent it."* If God speaks, and His word does not prevail, then He is not God! God has to speak in order for His words to manifest in whatever medium He chooses to operate in. His word will never return to Him void. Speak the word to your situations, and it shall prevail. Whether other words are spoken or not, His word shall stand, for He said His word will never return to Him empty. Now, as a messenger of God, learn to speak His words in the midst of adversities, for when you come out from the presence of those opposing your destiny, it will be known that a prophet was among their midst. People cannot overcome God's word; their actions against God's words are empty and without meaning. Choose to become a believer who declares God's word in his or her situation without fear, for the one who sent you to your destiny is greater than your circumstance. In the midst of that pain speak what will bring you joy; let this become your attitude concerning what is intending to conquer your dreams and vision.

Have You Lost Your Way?

Genesis 37:15–16: *"And a man found him wandering in the fields. And the man asked him, 'What are you seeking?' 'I am seeking my brothers,' he said. 'Tell me, please, where they are pasturing the flock.'"*

There are times in life when you can't find the exact route that you should travel on as you head toward your destiny. When Joseph was travelling to look for his brothers, he lost his way, and he began to wander in the fields. As he was wandering, a certain man found him in the fields. It was the man who found Joseph, and not Joseph who found the man; this means that Joseph did not seek help for himself, but a man suddenly appeared to guide him. Many questions may arise from that. Who was this man? Why was he fully informed about what Joseph was looking for? If this man did not pass there, could Joseph have found his way? A simple answer to all of these questions is that God sent a provision for Joseph. His needs were met unexpectedly. Joseph had a divine encounter through this strange man. The timing was so precise, for God was waiting for the moment at which confusion would take over Joseph's life. Joseph was predestined for greatness, and his destiny was guaranteed. It did not matter the state of mind he found himself in at that particular time. God devised whatever means necessary to guarantee joseph would walk into what He intended of him.

The man who gave Joseph his direction was not named in the passage, and yet he played a major role in Joseph's finding his brothers. Similarly, the

Lord knows that, at some point in your walk, you will wander around in the fields having no clue what step to take next. It was no coincidence that the strange man encountered Joseph, and so has God prepared everything for you. Every person assigned by God for your elevation is His way of arranging your success.

Some people are in the field wondering if ever they will get married. Others wonder if they will be employed, and some wonder if they will ever have children. Most believers pray to God, but do not experience any visible progress. Be still and know that the heavens themselves are not still. The Lord knew about your matter before you recognized it. Wait, for God is busy working something unique for you. What were the chances of Joseph meeting up with someone in the field? It was unlikely that he would meet anyone, let alone a person who had information about what he was looking for. In the field, God located Joseph, and a stranger navigated him into fulfilling his dreams. God has the ability to locate you, in that field of yours, where there is no address. God will send you a message …a word of direction to guide you to your future. It is not about who you know but it's about what God knows …people who don't exist in your vocabulary.

Luke 24:13–16: *"That very day two of them were going to a village named Emmaus, about seven miles from Jerusalem, and they were talking with each other about all these things that had happened. While they were talking and discussing together, Jesus himself drew near and went with them. But their eyes were kept from recognizing Him."*

Let it be your prayer that your eyes will not be kept from recognizing the Lord as He orchestrates and moves in your life. God answers, and in all that we do, we need to open our spiritual eyes in order to see Him as He operates. One thing interesting about the two men who were talking on their way to Emmaus is that they were talking about Jesus, and they did not recognize that it was Him they were talking to. In their speech they spoke well of Him. In Luke 24:19 one of them said to Him, *"Concerning Jesus of Nazareth, a man who was a prophet mighty in deed and word before God and all the people."*

Even if these men did not recognize Jesus, they did not utter a single word of blasphemy and dishonor against Jesus. What they spoke about Christ only honored Him and testified to how they personally viewed Him. When you are busy wondering how your next step in life will unfold, be cautious as well of how you talk about Him who is mighty in deeds, and do your best to be positively expectant.

Sometimes when you walk about in your neighborhood, you might assume that you are familiar with the people you come across. Little do you know, however, that some people are assigned by God for your breakthrough. The moment you open your mind, you will realize that some people are positioned by God around you for your well-being, and when you don't just pass them by, the Lord may use that small talk with them to settle your life-long disputes. It might even not be your intention to disclose your personal ideas to your neighbor, but somehow during your encounter with them, the Lord will drop your solution into your spirit. Sometimes conversations with strangers can take you to an unexpected turn in life.

Each and every person you come across carries a certain ability to uplift you; it does not matter how you relate or how you well know one another. Bad people help us to endure, and good people encourage us. Therefore, as we seek solutions to our day-to-day walk with the Lord, let us not ignore the ministration of strangers.

Matthew 25:38: *"And when did we see you a stranger and welcome you ..."*

Strangers are people you don't know yet, and one thing is evident: we are all a stranger to someone.

Second Corinthians 1:12: *"For our boast is this, the testimony of our conscience, that we behaved in the world with simplicity and godly sincerity, not by earthly wisdom but by the grace of God, and supremely so toward you."*

In this quote, the Apostle Paul is writing to the church of Corinth. In his message, he mentions the one important aspect in the nature of relationships, and that is the virtue of a person who speaks and acts openly his thoughts and desires. We have to desire that God-given frankness and sincerity, for it attracts men and women who hold the keys to the next leg of our journey.

In your relationships with people, allow God's wisdom to prevail rather than human wisdom, for what you see with your eyes might be different to what is reflected in the spirit arena. If you choose to interact with only those people who meet up with your earthly standards, you might miss the movement of the Lord and ultimately fall short from the intent of God in your lives.

When Joseph was wandering in the fields, the man asked him, *"What are you seeking?"* (Genesis 37:15).

If you knew that you were in need, and a stranger asked you that question, how would you openly and honestly respond? Probably some believers would not even bother to respond, especially if a person they didn't know had asked the question.

They would fail to respond in accordance to their faith; in other words, they would not take a step of faith to believe in their heart that this question was actually asked by God. They would not recognize that, if they answered well, then the Lord would respond well. Have a "kingdom mentality." Before your problems are resolved, seek first the righteousness of God's kingdom.

Matthew 6:33: *"But seek first the kingdom of God and his righteousness, and all these things will be added to you."*

How are you seeking God's righteousness? Is it not about doing good and expecting good even if the circumstances don't allow? Are you not expecting some people to be righteous? And when you seek righteousness, how will you know where to find it? If you don't make it your business to seek righteousness everywhere you go, you might miss God's kingdom, and when you miss God's kingdom, you have missed everything including your purpose.

Are you wandering in the field seeking direction as you look for what will profit you in life? Then God's kingdom is at hand. God's kingdom will not come one day, but it has come already, and it is in you. As long as you make God's kingdom a priority, your relationship with others will never be a problem. You will see every situation as a tunnel for elevation, and whom so ever you come across will become a potential candidate who can contribute something meaningful to your life. You will begin to understand that the Lord can use anyone and any situation you are not familiar with to promote you to greater heights. In most cases, people who have the largest influence in turning your dreams into a reality are the people you don't know.

Joseph said to the stranger, *"Tell me, please, where they are pasturing the flock"* (Genesis 37:16).

If Joseph had a hardened heart, it could have been evident from his response, but his heart was softened, and he knew that anybody could become a point of contact to help him reach his destiny. It is from his response that we learn that we can sometimes rely on people we don't know to give us guidance and direction toward our destiny. When you are destined for greatness, your story is not like the stories of the rest, and the only thing you undermine is impossibilities, because you understand that possibilities are your biggest inspiration. Men and woman of greater vision do not underestimate the qualities that God has placed on individuals, for they know that anybody can be God's treasure of hope for someone.

Deuteronomy 6:15: *"For the Lord your God in your midst is a jealous God."*

Some people you know believe that they hold your blessings, and these are people God does not use; instead, He chooses to use unexpected or unknown or unrelated individuals to abolish that mentality and also to save you from thinking that it is your "correct" way of doing things that made it possible for you to accomplish your vision.

First Corinthians 2:14–16: *"The natural person does not accept the things of the Spirit of God, for they are folly to him, and he is not able to understand them because they are spiritually discerned. The spiritual person judges all things, but is himself to be judged by no one. 'For who has understood the mind of the Lord so as to instruct him?'"*

Unspiritual people cannot comprehend spiritual things, which are folly to them. Spiritual people are able to discern their season of success. They become aware of the possibilities in the midst of lack. They cherish whatever they are offered, because they understand that it is not what their eyes see that makes things to happen for them, but it is all about the Lord of mysteries … the one who makes a way in the wilderness.

The word of God encourages us to be spiritual, for it is in the spirit where our true nature lies. The word says, *"For who has understood the mind of the Lord"* (1 Corinthians 2:16).

You cannot comprehend the mind of the Lord, and you cannot define the magnitude of His blessings for you, and you cannot measure the extent of His favor upon your life. If only you could describe how you will acquire your prosperity, then His influence would not be necessary. But because no man understands the mind of the Lord, you should always be prepared, because God is capable of appointing whomever He desires to usher you through your long-awaited door of greatness. The wisdom of God is for those who want to inherit His blessings. First Corinthians 2:7: *"But we impart a secret and hidden wisdom of God, which God decreed before the ages for our glory."*

One interesting factor about God's wisdom is that it is hidden, and yet can be imparted. If God really wanted to impart His wisdom to us, why is He hiding it from us? You see, God does not force anything on anyone. Additionally, what you don't make an effort to attain, you will not cherish. This means that discernment and wisdom are important attributes for you to possess when you are dealing with people or circumstances you are not familiar with. When the wisdom is hidden, some will not have access to it, for they will not aspire to seek it. And when they don't aspire to seek God's wisdom, they become unspiritual. God's ways seem unnatural to them. They do not believe that spiritual matters exist, and hence they walk only by what they can see, and not by faith.

There are three attributes that are significant tools you can use to assist you to determine and make predictions about what the Lord wants you to do when you encounter people you do not know or when you come across circumstances you are not familiar with. These three attributes represent God working in totality as the Holy Trinity, and they are:

1. Having the mind of the Lord (First Corinthians 2:16: *"But we have the mind of Christ."*)
2. Having a spiritual discernment (First Corinthians 2:14: *"They are spiritually discerned."*)
3. Having God's wisdom (First Corinthians 2:7: *"But we impart a secret and hidden wisdom of God."*)

Therefore, when you possess these attributes, it does not matter whom you meet. What is important is whom you go with. When you are equipped with these godly attributes, you will be led into the right associations, and the appointed people you meet will not delay to connect you to your God-given assignment. In short, God gives you the mind of Christ, and through Christ you acquire wisdom, and the Holy Spirit will guide you to the right channels God has destined for you through man and circumstances.

Chapter 3

Acts of the Devil

The Devil Sees You coming from Afar

Genesis 37:18: *"They saw him from afar, and before he came near to them they conspired against him to kill him."*

Joseph's brothers conspired against him the moment they saw him coming. They plotted evil against him long before he came into their midst. They associated him with his dreams, and the closer he came to them, the more they saw the dreams come to pass.

Are you having a particular vision and you want to see yourself bringing it to existence? If so, the devil has seen your potential from afar. He heard it when the word of God was preached to you, and you believed every single part of it. And he saw how you put that word into practice irrespective of all manner of circumstances. That word became alive in you, and you were consumed by it and developed a zeal for the ways of the Lord in speech and deeds. These things made the devil furious, for his wish is to see you failing to know and live your divine assignment here on earth. This causes the devil to raise adversities against you, to hinder you from accomplishing your dreams. When the devil sees you, he sees your gifts in use. He sees you leading your family out of captivity. He sees you shining the light of God among those in darkness. He sees your bright future and your joyful stories of God's grace upon your life. One thing you should do is keep on walking, not by your own strength or understanding, but by God's guidance.

John 11:17–20: *"Now when Jesus came, he found that Lazarus had already been in the tomb four days. Bethany was near Jerusalem, about two miles off, and many of the Jews had come to Martha and Mary to console them concerning their brother. So when Martha heard that Jesus was coming, she went and met him, but Mary remained seated in the house."*

John 11:37: *"But some of them [Jews] said, 'Could not he who opened the eyes of the blind man also have kept this man from dying?'"*

Before Jesus could even begin with the miracle of raising Lazarus from the dead, some Jews already concluded that He had failed to keep Lazarus from dying.

Martha heard that Jesus was coming, and whilst He was on His way, the gathering began to be divided in opinion. There were those who were eagerly expecting to see the actions of God and those who doubted what God would do. Those who doubted God's glory already did not see the need for Jesus to come, because to them there was nothing Jesus could do at that particular moment.

If Martha had taken their doubt into consideration, she would not have welcomed Jesus into their home and appreciated His presence. This, however, was not going to prevent Jesus from glorifying the name of the Lord, because it was the will of God to raise Lazarus despite their unbelief.

Visions are undermined before they are conceived, dreams are shuttered before they are lived, missions are scattered before they are achieved, and lives are destroyed before they are experienced. Who on earth is able to prevent the will of God from being established in your life? What circumstance is so huge that God is invisible in it? The doubt of man cannot prevent Him from performing mighty deeds, and the Lord does not have any spot of fear in Him to accomplish what He wants to accomplish in your life.

Exodus 14:8–10: *"And the Lord hardened the heart of Pharaoh King of Egypt, and He pursued the people of Israel while the people of Israel were going out defiantly. The Egyptians pursued them, all Pharaoh's horses and chariots and his horsemen and his army, and overtook them encamped at the sea, by Pi-hahiroth, in front of Baal-zephon Pihahiroth. When Pharaoh drew near, the people of Israel lifted up their eyes, and behold, the Egyptians were marching after them, and they feared greatly. And the people of Israel cried out to the Lord."*

When the children of Israel left Egypt, they became resistant to fear, for their time had come. And when they had travelled a certain distance from Egypt, the king changed his mind concerning their freedom, and the Egyptians pursued God's children. They saw the future of God's children from afar. They saw what a mighty nation they would became and how they would begin to enjoy their freedom. They saw the Israelites from afar.

The further the Israelites walked away from their place of bondage, the more they weakened those who had kept them in captivity. Usually what happens is that most people receive their breakthrough but not their freedom. The devil cannot do without them; hence, whenever they are set free from bondage and addiction, the devil does not surrender, but reinforces and comes after them. What is the cause of this? Why can't he just let it all go? That would not be easy for him, because you know how he operates, and you will later attack his kingdom with his schemes. One would ask, then, why is he releasing you at all? The devil is forced by God to release you; meanwhile, his heart remains hardened. It is not his will to set you free, and yet he has no choice but to set you free for your elevation and your promotion. This is where God comes in with a miracle, at the time when your freedom is being challenged and threatened. You need Pharaoh's army to come back in order to see the hand of the Lord. You cannot see your destiny unless you see your total freedom. There has to be a place you remember, and when you do, you conclude who wanted to deny you your breakthrough. Exodus 14:13: *"The Egyptians whom you see today, you shall never see again."*

When you look behind you, you will see from afar as well, and you will plead to the Lord for your miracle, for you will understand that, if you don't get it, you will be taken into captivity once more, or maybe you will be destroyed. The look you should have toward conspiracy and those seeking to make you captive should be the look of faith in God. The devil knows that he has made a big mistake by releasing you to see your true identity and allowing you to taste your freedom, because the dreams you have long carried are now becoming a reality. The moment you seize your freedom you have seized your own uplifting.

Jeremiah 11:18: *"The Lord made it known to me and I knew; then you showed me their deeds. But I was like a gentle lamb led to the slaughter. I did not know if it was against me they devised schemes, saying, 'Let us destroy the tree with its fruit, let us cut him off from the land of the living, that his name be remembered no more.'"*

These are the schemes of evil people concerning your life—merciless people devising evil deeds for the tree and its fruit, meaning that the devil is after you and all that you bear. One would ask, does such evil exist that causes people to devise schemes to cut you off from the land of the living, even if you haven't done anything to them? Absolutely. Jeremiah experienced this kind of evil; people conspired against him to cut him off from the land of the living.

Jeremiah 12:6: *"For even your brothers and the house of your father, even they have dealt treacherously with you; they are in full cry after you; do not believe them, though they speak friendly words to you."*

The Good News Translation of this verse goes like this: *"Even your relatives, members of your own family, have betrayed you; they join in the attacks against you. Do not trust them, even though they speak friendly words."*

Not only are your enemies distant people from you, but these are members of your father's house …your relatives. They are the people who want your name to be cut off from the land of the living. They see the beautiful fruits produced by the tree, and they do not want other people to enjoy the fruits after harvest. It is interesting to know the reasons propelling these people to act in such evil against your life.

Your life is like a fruitful tree. This means that you are the type of a person who is rooted in what the Lord has mandated for you, and you have the ability to stand in all seasons of life without falling to the ground. You are able to survive any form of conditions you find yourself in, and as each season comes, you stand and wait for another season to come, until all four seasons—the hot, the cold, the windy, and the calm seasons—have all taken their course over your life.

The fruit you bear represents your productivity, prosperity, and growth. You are a tree that does not only stand, but you are a tree that stands for a cause—to produce fruit. People can see progress, growth, and prosperity in your life. There is a spiritual growth taking place; your spiritual channels are no longer blocked, there is a flow of God's spirit in you, and this makes you productive as you instill God's presence in those in need of it. Whatever you lay your hands to succeeds and prospers, for you are productive.

Your name is important. Jeremiah's brother wanted his name to be forgotten, never to be remembered by his generation. But why were they interested in the name? What role and effect did he have that made people even want to forget his name? Well, this shows that Jeremiah was a man of influence. People saw what he carried, and all the qualities he possessed that enabled him to be great. Hence they declared that his name should never more be remembered, because they did not want any generation to ever pronounce and declare him their deliverer.

Jeremiah is a major prophet in the book of life, and today and for generations to come people will always refer to the word of God through his life. This is what the devil saw coming; he wanted the name of Jeremiah never to be remembered. Jeremiah's life was not only recorded in any book, it was recorded in the Bible, the Book of Life. Never will his name be forgotten. The devil was aware that God was going to use Jeremiah to write His word, and he also knew that the word of the Lord through Jeremiah would make a great impact in drawing people to the Lord; hence, he wanted to cut Jeremiah from the land of the living before he acquired his mandate.

The devil knows your outcome as well. That is why he wants to do the same thing to you that he tried to do to Jeremiah. But just as he did not succeed in Jeremiah's life, so shall he not succeed with yours. You will be a tree planted by the water, and you will bear fruit. Your name will be remembered from generation to generation not only by your community, but by the entire world.

The devil can see from afar into your future, and he will try whatever means possible to hinder you. He knows that you are the next great prophet or prophetess, a soul winner who will perform mighty deeds and whose name will never be forgotten by generations till Jesus comes.

Jeremiah never promoted his name, and yet his name became a threat to the enemy. He never campaigned to be a great man, but God elevated him to a high place because of the schemes the enemy had toward him. Whenever the devil pronounces something evil against you to prevent you from seeing your destiny, God will counteract that effort by fulfilling His promises in your life. Don't sell yourself to the enemy by being intimidated, for the Lord is your helper. Do not force your way into great and higher places, for He will take you there-by Himself. Let it not be your habit to associate with great people, for great people will make it their habit to associate with you.

Any attempt by the enemy to cut you out of the land of the living will guarantee you a wealthy, healthy, long life in Christ Jesus.

You need not talk. Simply look on as the Lord uses the same axe the devil planned to use against you to cut off their association with you. In Jeremiah 13:18 we read: *"Say to the king and the queen mother: "Take a lowly seat, for your beautiful crown has come down from your head.""* The Good News Bible says, *"Beautiful crowns have fallen from their heads."* This is an involuntarily act by the king and queen to take off their crowns, because the crowns fell by themselves; they were not removed by anyone. This act is an unwillingly one to the king and the queen. The crowns just fell off their heads unaided by human hands. This is a sign that the kings and queens hindering your destiny have no choice but to be enthroned away from their authorities. The order of the royal family has changed; no more are there rulers who seek your downfall; no more are there authorities who seek your destruction. This time God is changing a particular trend of a certain royal family that has been a problem for your future. The Lord is taking the crowns of your oppressors from their heads and putting them onto yours. There is an involuntarily act from the king and queen's mother. The Lord is forcing them to make a way for you to be great.

The Lord said to Jeremiah, *"If you have raced with men on foot, and they have wearied you, how will you compete with horses?"* (Jeremiah 12:5).

The evil schemes of man should not worry you, because God expects you to outrun every wickedness designed to bring you down. The Lord has instilled in you all the necessary weapons of warfare so that you can conquer evil every step of the way. That evil, which is designed to doom your future, is nothing compared to what you carry inside of you. When the Lord was speaking to Jeremiah concerning this matter, He was simply saying that the evil Jeremiah said was worrying him did not even match the capacity and the magnitude of vigor bestowed in him to silence every voice raised up high to condemn the works of his hand. God was not expecting Jeremiah to crumble and fall apart whenever evil rose up against him seeking his flesh, for Jeremiah understood better than anyone else that God was the giver of life, and no one else.

Anybody planning evil against you can never outrun you. What the Lord has made you to be cannot be compared to what they are. Allow them to carry on with their evil, and continue with your steps. Even as you walk you are destabilizing their plans. Your presence in their midst shatters every arrow of destruction directed to you. When you open your mouth to talk, your voice will resurrect every dead dream they intended to bury, and your declarations will manifest. Allow and give them space and time to lay their traps where you will walk, and all their efforts will be in vain. You are not their equal. You are carrying God, and they are walking in evil. What does evil have that will overcome what the Lord has? It is nothing, and because it is nothing before the Lord, so shall it be before you. Decide how you want to walk to your destiny—in fear or with boldness! And know that you have what it takes to compete with horses, meaning that you can even outrun what was created to run faster. And if you can run faster than a horse, nothing will stand in your way to becoming crowned victorious. Come out and carry yourself up. Be prepared and get ready. You are on your way to outrunning all forms of evil plotted against you. Sickness cannot make you weary, and no amount of difficulty can suppress what the Lord Almighty has placed in you.

When Covering Is Removed

Genesis 37:20–22 *"Come now, let us kill him and throw him into one of the pits. Then we will say that a fierce animal has devoured him, and we will see what will become of his dreams.' But when Reuben heard it, he rescued him out of their hands, saying, 'Let us not take his life.' And Rueben said to them, 'Shed no blood; throw him into this pit here in the wilderness, but do not lay a hand on him'—that he might rescue him out of their hand to restore him to his father. So when Joseph came to his brothers, they stripped him of his robe, the robe of many colors that he wore."*

As a believer, you wear a covering over your life. In Joseph's story, it is represented by the robe of many colors he wore. A covering is an attribute of God that is found on His children. It is a spiritual cloth of uniqueness wrapped around you to qualify you to possess what God wants you to possess. Your integrity, your gifts, and God's glory are special features of divine capacity that live in you, and these features are easily noticeable to the enemy. That is why he is after you. This became evident when Joseph's brothers envied the robe that he wore and sought to take it from him. This is what the enemy is after—the robe of God on you. The enemy has every intention of stripping you of the glory of God—taking away your God-given potential and throwing you into a pit. God's light is seen on each and every believer, and this is one of the colors of your robe.

Your abilities are your beauty. They make you who you are; they brighten up your life, and this is what bothers other people. The enemy does not want to see brightness in your life; that brightness disturbs and disrupts the enemy's mission. Evil does not want to see your talents exercised to glorify the Lord, and all those who welcome it hate transparency. Jacob chose Joseph as the one he wanted to wear that robe, and this offended Joseph's brothers. This is the nature of special gifts; it exposes the evil nature hidden in some people you are associated with. Do you have special gifts and talents the Lord has blessed you with? Do you possess things that others do not have? Then the devil will attempt to remove that covering from you.

Daniel 5:12: *"Because an excellent spirit, knowledge, and understanding to interpret dreams, explain riddles, and solve problems were found in this Daniel."*

Daniel had many spiritual gifts from the Lord; they made up the garment the Lord gave to him to wear. With such qualities, Daniel could govern the whole nation alone. And these qualities would make others envy who he was rather than learning and appreciating what God had instilled in him. One of the colors that stood out from his garment was the gift of problem solving. This gift enabled Daniel to expose evil schemes and to provide personal intervention to assist those in need of solutions. He was able to put an end to the tormenting spirits that inflicted confusion and hardship in people's lives. He managed to resolve all problems he encountered. And because Daniel had this God-given gift, evildoers never acknowledged it. In all that Daniel did, excellence would be the end result.

Those who wear the robe of many colors, which represents the numerous gifts any individual possesses, rely only on the one who gave them that garment, and that is the Lord. They depend only on the Lord, for it is He who works in them, and causes all human efforts raised to seize their services to become invalid.

An excellent spirit was one of the colors found in the garment worn by Daniel. This spirit works in all areas of our lives as we pursue our destinies. It settles every dispute, and it unfolds and perfects every effort of man to accomplish his mandate in all that he does. You need an excellent spirit in order to succeed in all spiritual endeavors, and what you should know is that the enemy will attempt to hinder every task you put your hands to.

Revelations 3:11: *"I am coming soon. Hold fast what you have, so that no one may seize your crown."*

In this lifetime there are those who seek the crown you are wearing. They want to seize it by removing the garment of the Lord, which is made up of the gifts the Lord has given you. The Lord is pleading with you to hold fast to your crown so that evil men do not seize what He has placed in you.

Job 1:1: *"There was a man in the land of Uz whose name was Job, and that man was blameless and upright, one who feared God and turned away from evil."*

These are the attributes of Job. He wore a unique robe of many colors, which represented the gifts of God in his life. What does it take today for a man to be blameless and walk on the surface of the earth without any crookedness? It takes only the fear of the Lord, which is the dominant color on any man's garment. The fear of the Lord paves the way for man in all his endeavors. It sustains the relationship between a believer and God; His nature is understood by those who fear Him, and others recognize that. As a believer, fear the Lord and put on this garment. People like him who fear the Lord with all their being are the ones who face all sorts of atrocities of life. This is because the enemy is at work trying to remove these attributes from them. To such individuals who have godly attributes, the devil will formulate all sorts of evil schemes to bring them to a point where they will just be left with no choice but to surrender and allow the covering to be removed from them. When all temptations of the devil have been paraded through your life, and the eyes of the wicked are awaiting your last breath, there is only one thing that you do not have to consider, and that is to surrender the robe that the Lord has blessed you with, hold it fast, and never let it go. Do not allow members of the evil camp to take it off, for the qualities that you have are a gateway to your destiny.

Luke 2:40: *"And the child [Jesus] grew and became strong, filled with wisdom. And the favor of God was upon him."*

Jesus also wore a unique garment of many colors. What made this garment more attractive than any other was the fact that, as he grew, the garment became brighter and brighter, and more attractive. When wisdom has reached its peak, it attracts multitudes, and among the multitudes, those who envy your garment will seek an opportunity to remove it from you.

One of the dominant colors on the robe worn by Jesus was the favor of the Lord. The Lord's favor unlocks doors that cannot be opened by others. The favor of the Lord makes ways in the seas, and it proclaims defeat over your enemies before you enter in battle with them. His favor disqualifies the proud and grants the humble victory. It limits the strengths of armies and regards the words of the wicked as null and the silent whispers of the righteous as shouts of the multitude.

Romans 8:15: *"For you did not receive the spirit of slavery to fall back into fear, but you have received the Spirit of adoption as sons, by whom we cry, 'Abba! Father!'"*

Those who are chosen by the Lord to put on the unique robe of inheritance of God's spiritual attitudes should not fall back in fear. When the enemy surrounds you and claims the glory of the Lord over your life, refuse to surrender your garment. Say no to his intimidating actions and cry out to your Father, from whom you have received the spirit of adoption as sons and daughters. Cry, "Abba! Father!" Do not allow the devil to take off the robe that the Lord has given you to wear. Cry out, "Lord, my Father, I do not want to fall back into fear, for I have received the spirit of adoption, and whatever evil schemes coming against my life to take from me the gifts of God in my life should all fail!"

First John 5:4: *"For everyone who has been born of God overcomes the world. And this is the victory that has overcome the world—our faith."*

Your faith enables you to be victorious in all battles with evil raised against your success and against your future. It overcomes the world. This means that you are given the world to rule over, and it is not possible for the world to overcome those who should rule over it. Your faith makes it possible for you to overcome those who seek to remove the covering of the Lord over your life. Only you must have this understanding: there are no evil circumstances designed to conquer what God has given birth to. No person can determine the fate of how your faith will work for you. And through your faith, you can nullify every work of evil pronounced against your life.

Overcome the schemes of evil plotted against you by the words of faith that come out of your mouth. Faith is always weighed by the Lord, and not by man. People do not determine the level of faith you possess, and they cannot predict its outcome. Faith is measured only by the Lord, and from Him come the results of it. God is the only one who is pleased by your faith, and no counsel is sought to validate its sufficiency. Therefore, faith is a language you should learn to speak to God alone, for He is the only one that understands that language. This means that the voice of man does not hold any meaningful influence in God's decision about your outcome; you alone can access your victorious mandate through faith to establish every good intention you have on earth.

Faith does not have to increase in abundance. You don't need a huge amount of faith to live to your vision; in other words, a little faith is a lot of faith before the Lord; as long as it is faith, it is a total measure of faith given to you for you to use to please God. One step of faith is a total measure of the faith the Lord has granted to you. Faith is never "enough" or "a minimum." Any measure of it is appropriate. Only one thing disqualifies faith, and that is doubt. Therefore, we should always practice activating the faith given to us by the Lord. That will ensure that all our victories will be guaranteed.

Hebrews 9:11–14: *"But when Christ appeared as a high priest of the good things that has come, then through the greater and more perfect tent (not made with hands, that is, not of this creation) he entered once for all into the holy places, not by means of the blood of goats and calves but by means of his own blood, thus serving eternal redemption. For if the blood of goats and bulls, and the sprinkling of defiled persons with the ashes of a heifer, sanctify for the purification of the flesh, how much more will the blood of Christ, who through the eternal Spirit offered himself without blemish to God, purify our conscience from dead works to serve the living God."*

The blood of Jesus is a multifunctional garment suitable for all occasions, and when you cover yourself with that blood, you are putting on a special garment of many colors. This is a garment that you should wear at all times. It is the garment of victory worn by victorious people, and by those whose conscience is set free from dead works.

It is through this robe of the blood of the lamb that your services to the Lord will make it possible for the Lord to intervene whenever enemies gather against you to remove the covering of the Lord. They do this because they know that, with God's covering, limitation will only be a hopeful echo sounding in the minds of those seeking your downfall.

Jesus entered once and for all into the holy places. He did not need any consultation from man to be sure that He would successfully make it the first time into the holy place. He was sure that He was a true sacrifice without any blemish, and no evil would hinder Him from entering there. Similarly He wants you to be sure of your entry into your destiny. The Lord will silence the gathering of the wicked who demand your flesh once and for all. Through the blood of Christ, every evil being seeking your soul will be put to shame, and no arrow will enter your courts; rather, your arrows will pursue and accomplish their mission in the camp of evil.

Shed No Blood

Because of the blood of Jesus Christ, not a drop of blood will come from your body. When Joseph's brothers wanted to kill him, one of his brothers refused any bloodshed.

Genesis 37:22: *"And Reuben said to them, 'Shed no blood.'"*

Reuben protected Joseph from being sacrificed. He did not allow his brothers to shed his blood. Jesus Himself was a sacrifice raised by God to protect you from those who demand your blood. Christ is the only sacrifice, and none of His children will suffer bloodshed. Once and for all, He went into the holy places to become a sacrifice for those who are called by His name.

Hebrews 9:12: *"He entered once for all into the holy places, not by means of the blood of goats and calves but by means of his own blood, thus securing an eternal redemption."*

Because Jesus shed His own blood, there became no need for sacrificing goats and calves. There was no need for any man to shed his blood in sacrifice. It is through His blood that He rescued your destiny from the hands of the wicked, securing your future through His blood. The blood of Jesus unlocks every channel that leads you to the life of abundant supernatural supply. To secure something is to set it aside and make reservations as to what it will be used for in times to come. This is what Christ has done. He has prepared and set aside all things you will use in times to come. The visions you have are just the beginning of where the Lord is taking you, and they complement what He has already made you to be and to have in times to come. In other words, Christ has secured your future and it has been prepared; it is awaiting your vision to unfold in order for you to live your life to its maximum capacity.

The blood of Jesus protects you from every evil against your life. When you put it on it becomes a covering that no evil will penetrate. It will *"purify our conscience from dead works to serve the living God"* (Hebrews 9:14).

There is no dead circumstance that the blood of Jesus cannot resurrect. Put on that covering, which is the blood of Christ, and whatever vision of greatness you carry will come to pass, and it shall excel.

In the Pit

Genesis 37:24: *"And they took him and threw him into a pit. The pit was empty; there was no water in it."*

A pit is a place where the devil desires to put each and every person the Lord wants to embrace. When you are thrown into a deep pit, there is very little that you can do to save yourself. Those who are dragged into a pit are usually overpowered and outnumbered by those who seek to put an end to their lives. Joseph's brothers were all older than him, and it is possible that they were also big in stature; therefore, it is quite evident that it would not be difficult for them to cast him into a pit. Joseph was helpless, and his life was in the hands of his brothers. He could do nothing about the matter, but just surrender himself to them. There are times in life when the devil rises in ambush against your life … times when the people you hold in high regard gather themselves and outnumber you as you pursue your life's dreams. Usually a person who is ambushed by the enemy and cast into the pit is seen to have a stagnant life. Spiritually, it's a life in which the fellowship with the Spirit has been lost and there is insufficient knowledge of the word of God. Inside a pit, there are limitations, and one cannot fulfill one's walk accordingly because of stagnation. The pit that Joseph was cast into was empty and did not have water. Water symbolizes the presence of the Holy Spirit, and emptiness is a symbol of lack of the knowledge of God's word. If you are a believer and you are experiencing emptiness and thirst, know that you are being ambushed by the enemy and you have been cast into the pit. Is there anything wrong with people who are ambushed into the pit? Nothing wrong; it is not their fault that they were suddenly attacked by those hiding or pretending to be brothers. It is not your fault when those you thought would upgrade your standings become your opposition. When all doors are closed, the zeal you have for the Lord is drained.

Christians who don't have an appetite for fellowship with the Spirit of the Lord and don't seek knowledge from His word are clearly cast into a pit. Second Timothy 2:15: *"Do your best to present yourself to God as one approved a worker who has no need to be ashamed, rightly handling the word of truth."*

When times of emptiness and dryness enter your spirit, you have to work your way out of it to the best of your ability and present to God what would please Him. God does not demand anyone to do anything beyond what He expects of him or her, but instead He expects each one of us to follow what will make us approved by Him in all that we want to pursue. The best way to do that is to rightfully handle His word. When the enemy has opened all channels of tribulation into your life, do your best to show yourself approved before God. In the midst of travail and confusion, become a worker who takes care of his affairs truthfully without being ashamed of God's word. And the moment you begin to rightfully handle the word of truth, the Lord will rightfully handle the things you could not handle. The word of God is a key. We must give God access to handle our lives and stand in against situations and circumstances that rise to challenge our lives.

Romans 8:26: *"The Spirit helps us in our weakness."* If only you will rely on the word of God and hope for God's intervention, the Spirit will also help you in your weakness, and as a result, your enemies will be put to shame, and their deeds will not succeed in negatively influencing your life. God knows that sometimes immortal beings can become very weak and overcome by terror and fear, but in all that what matters most is how you handle His word. This is what determines the outcome of your challenges. When you are in a pit, God is not only looking on, but He is preparing and creating a way out for you, and the only thing that will make Him keep on working is the way you continually handle His word. If you are dry spiritually, it is just a matter of time before everything will be dry. Your finances and the work of your hands will also be affected, and you will ultimately not experience the peace and joy of the Lord.

Second Samuel 21:15: *"There was war again between the Philistines and Israel, and David went down together with his servants, and they fought against the Philistines. And David grew weary. And Ishbi-benob, one of the descendants of the giants, whose spear weighed three hundred shekels of bronze, and who was armed with a new sword, thought to kill David. But Abishaithe son of Zeruiah came to his aid and attacked the Philistine and killed him."*

It does not matter how weak and how defenseless you may be, just as it did for David, a defense will come from the Lord. A solution will suddenly appear, and the Lord will come to your aid. God Himself will defend you when you least expect it. It does not matter how weak and terrified you are; what matters is that, in your weakness, your need will be meet. David thought his life had ended, but it was a beginning of his testimony. Even if there is nothing that seems to be working out for you, and the enemy is just about to finish what he began, with the same attitude the Lord will strike them before their evil is accomplished. The giant Ishbi-benob had to be armed with a new sword in order to strike David. He took the battle with David very seriously—to such an extent that he brought out a new sword, one that had never been used before. It does not matter how organized the devil may be against you, every new trick and every new strategy and every new piece of armor that is used against your life will be pronounced useless by the Lord. Help will not cease to come, solutions will not run out, and the strength of the Lord will not fade. He will not struggle in His rescue of your life from those who are allies against your destiny.

First Samuel 14:24–30: *"And the men of Israel had been hard pressed that day, so Saul had laid an oath on the people, saying, 'Cursed be the man who eats food until it is evening and I am avenged on my enemies.' So none of the people had tasted food. Now when all the people came to the forest, behold, there was honey on the ground. And when the people entered the forest, behold, the honey was dropping, but no one put his hand to his mouth, for the people feared the oath. But Jonathan had not heard his father charge the people with the oath, so he put out the tip of the staff that was in his hand and dipped it in the honeycomb and put his hand to his mouth, and his eyes became bright. Then one of the people said, 'Your father strictly charged the people with an oath, saying, "Cursed be the man who eats food this day."' And the people were faint. Then Jonathan said, 'My father has troubled the land. See how my eyes have become bright because I tasted a little of this honey. How much better if the people had eaten freely today of the spoil of their enemies that they found. For now the defeat among the Philistines has not been great.'"*

Most of our victories in life have not been great, simply because we are faint. We fight our battles in fatigue, with minimum power to fight back over the enemy. Even if we shout, "Victory, victory!" the victory itself is not to the greatest extent. This makes the enemy regroup and assemble another battle to overcome us.

What made Jonathan miss the pronouncement of the oath of his father, Saul, that they should not taste food when going to battle? It was the Lord who strategically made Jonathan absent himself when the oath was pronounced, for He knew that the king's oath would reduce the chances of their success.

If Jonathan had been there when his father's oath was pronounced, he would have taken heed and he would have obeyed, and the secret to Israel's total supply of energy for battle would not have been revealed.

No matter the type of decree that has been made concerning your future and the state of weakness that you find yourself in, God has a way to boast you up and prepare you for your next big victory. When Saul spoke, the whole nation stood still and listened. God is saying to you today that all decrees made to disqualify you from your victory shall be scattered. You will not be a partaker of evil vows, and whatever pronouncement made on your behalf will be rendered useless before your path. There is no need for you to hear evil pronouncements made to hamper your source of strength, for the Lord God will be your ears, and He will not allow your enemy's words to come to pass in your life.

I Samuel 14:45: *"Then the people said to Saul, 'Shall Jonathan die'… far from it! As the Lord lives, there shall not one hair of his head fall to the ground, for he has worked with God this day."*

The people made it clear to King Saul that his son, Jonathan, was the one who had a good relationship with God rather than Saul. Jonathan did not announce his relationship with the Lord to the people, but the people themselves saw the works of God in his life and stood for him. Similarly, there will be no need for you to disclose your relationship with the Lord, but the people themselves will see the Lord at work in you. The very same enemies who are after your life will see God in action, defending against their evil deeds, and the name of the Lord shall be glorified. Saul's words were not accepted by the Lord even though he made a public vow that seemed to be coming from the Lord, but the people later noticed that what he had said was not from God. An alliance may be formed against your life. Nations can rise up against you. Floods can come up to your neck. The furnace may need to be adjusted to a great measure, and you may be put into the pit by those who are close to you, but when all that happens, proclaim the word in James 1:2: *"Count it all joy, my brothers, when you meet trials of various kinds, for you know that the testing of your faith produces steadfastness. And let steadfastness have its full effect, that you may be perfect and complete, lacking in nothing."*

Trading with Your Soul

Genesis 37:28: *"Then Midianite traders passed by. And they drew Joseph up and lifted him out of the pit, and sold him to the Ishmaelites for twenty shekels of silver. They took Joseph to Egypt."*

Some people willingly surrender their souls to the devil when they come across different challenges in life. They begin to lose hope from the only God and consciously sell their souls in exchange for a better life. Even if some are unconsciously dedicated, it is because of their lack of commitment to the true God that the devil manages to conquer them. They walk with no idea that they belong to a god elsewhere other than the true living God.

God had destined Joseph's blessing to be in Egypt, a place of bondage, but no conscious man would willingly allow himself to be in bondage in order to be blessed. Paving your way to greatness in exchange for your soul is a self-inflicted bondage that does not glorify the Lord. It is God Himself who allows man to be in bondage and in return delivers man to prosperity. It is not man who should sacrifice his soul to be in chains to acquire wealth.

Genesis 25:29–34: *"Once when Jacob was cooking stew, Esau came in from the field, and he was exhausted. And Esau said to Jacob, 'Let me eat some of that red stew, for I am exhausted!' (Therefore his name was called Edom.) Jacob said, 'Sell me your birthright now.' Esau said, 'I am about to die; of what use is a birthright to me?' Jacob said, 'Swear to me now.' So he swore to him and sold his birthright to Jacob. Then Jacob gave Esau bread and lentil stew, and he ate and drank and rose and went his way. Thus Esau despised his birthright."*

Esau sold his birthright for a meal, which he himself was supposed to provide because he was a hunter. The Lord equipped him with skills to hunt and supply game to his family. Genesis 25:27: *"Esau was a skilled hunter."*

But surprisingly he was the one who was in need, and he demanded food from the one who was not assigned with hunting skills.

This is what some skilled people do. They trade their valuables with individuals who don't have the skills they have.

Are you skilful and yet exhausted by hunger and poverty? Then use your skills to feed yourself. Use the gifts that God has blessed you with, and do not permit individuals who don't posses what you have to take advantage of you. Some people spend years in institutions of higher learning to prepare for a better living for their future, and when they are not employed after completing their studies, they sell themselves to anything that comes their way in desperation. Skilled people carry the blessings of the Lord, and there is a special grace in waiting for the opportune time to use them. It is only when they become vulnerable that the devil begins to offer them what they will later regret. Jesus told the following parable:

Luke 16:1: *"There was a rich man who had a manager, and charges were brought to him that this man was wasting his possessions. And he called him and said to him, 'What is this that I hear about you? Turn in the account of your management, for you can no longer be manager.' And the manager said to himself, 'What shall I do, since my master is taking the management away from me? I am not strong enough to dig, and I am ashamed to beg. I have decided what to do, so that when I am removed from management, people may receive me into their houses.' So, summoning his master's debtors one by one, he said to the first, 'How much do you owe my master?' He said, 'A hundred measures of oil.' He said to him, 'Take your bill, and sit down quickly and write fifty.' Then he said to another, 'And how much do you owe?' He said, 'A hundred measures of wheat.' He said to him, 'Take your bill, and write eighty.' The master commended the dishonest manager for his shrewdness. For the sons of this world are more shrewd in dealing with their own generation than the sons of light. And I tell you, make friends for yourselves by means of unrighteous wealth, so that when it fails they may receive you into the eternal dwellings. 'One who is faithful in a very little is also faithful in much, and one who is dishonest in a very little is also dishonest in much.'"*

Our generation has got some ignorant people who are led astray by others in the name of riches. The wheat and oil that the Lord Jesus spoke about in the parable represent day-to-day necessities. This, however, does not limit those who go to the extent of selling their birthright to fill their stomachs. Selling your soul to the devil requires sacrifices that will damage your relationship with your Lord Jesus Christ.

Nowadays souls are attached to wealth. People trade their birthrights by selling their identities in exchange for money; they sell one another like goods. In desperation, many allow their identities to be used to uplift those who want to pursue their personal agendas for their personal gain. Jesus said, in Luke 16:8: *"For the sons of this world are more shrewed in dealing with their own generation than the sons of light."*

This means that the sons of this world are quick in resolving their matters. They use their intellectuality to find solutions to their hardships, and they are better at devising a means to prosper than the sons of the light. Why is it like that? Does it mean that God is quicker to respond to their needs than He is to the needs of the sons of the light? Definitely not. The sons of this world don't rely on God, and they don't wait on Him or seek His face whenever they want to do anything. On the other hand, the sons of light wait only on the Lord to direct their steps. They can't take a single step before God says so, and God directs their destiny. They can do only one thing, and that is to seek His face and wait on Him in all that they do.

Luke 16:10: *"One who is faithful in very little is also faithful in much."*

Are you undermining the blessings you have? Does life mean nothing to you? Do you see no value in existing? Do not render yourself useless; rather than appreciate the life God has blessed you with, and use whatever talent He has given to you. That talent might be small or underestimated by others; just be faithful to it, and many more things will be given to you.

Remember what Esau did. He despised his birthright; to him it meant nothing. His age, his right to life, and being part of a family as a firstborn child meant nothing to him. This is what most of us do—we despise the very things that should make who we should be. We despise little things, and we fail to be honest in small matters. We don't become faithful over little things because, to us, little things mean nothing. But we forget that, to God, little things are huge. The promises of the Lord are as simple as He said: *"One who is faithful in a very little is also faithful in much"* (Luke 16:10).

Judges 16:15–17: *"And she said to him, 'How can you say, "I love you," when your heart is not with me? You have mocked me these three times, and you have not told me where your great strength lies.' And when she pressed him hard with her words day after day, and urged him, his soul was vexed to death. And he told her all his heart, and said to her, 'A razor has never come upon my head, for I have been a Nazirite to God from my mother's womb.'"*

Is there anything that is pressing you so hard that you are almost considering giving in? Samson sold himself to the Philistine woman because of love, which Delilah did not have for him. He did something that he never thought he would do; that is, he told an enemy the source of his might.

When the enemy is after your soul, he will not retreat easily. The enemy does not get weary in coming for what he wants from you. Just like Delilah, your enemy uses the same tactics over and over again until you decide to surrender. He comes over and over again with the same kind of deceptions, focusing on a particular target. The devil is very strategic in doing this; he chooses an area on which he will apply all his attention with the intention of making you ineffective in that area of your life. He chooses an area in a person's life that he knows he can use to take charge of that person's entire life. If your finances are the target, he will focus on bringing them down. If it is your marriage he is after, he will keep on bringing one matter up after the other to make you quit from it. He does not run around randomly without having an exact area of interest. He uses the access that he gets in a specific area to take charge of your entire life.

Ephesians 6:13: *"Therefore take up the whole amour of God, that you may be able to withstand in the evil day, and having done all, to stand firm."*

It is possible to withstand evil days. These days don't alert you when they are coming. That is the reason you should always put on the whole amour of the Lord. It is only when the belt of truth is girded around your waist that you can withstand temptation. Samson failed to be truthful to himself; that is why he ended up surrendering to Delilah. He failed to notice the numerous attempts made by Delilah to bring him down. This was because he was clouded with love, even though Delilah did not have the same feeling toward him. When you are truthful, you won't reveal the secrets that make you who you are. You can't allow your emotions to force you to expose that which the Lord has hidden in you. No matter who comes and how he comes, do not reveal the secrets the Lord has put into your life. You can reveal God's secrets by associating and giving in to those who do evil.

Philippians 1:27–28: *"Only let your manner of life be worthy of the gospel of Christ, so that whether I come and see you or am absent, I may hear of you that you are standing firm in one spirit, with one mind striving side by side for the faith of the gospel, and not frightened in anything by your opponents. This is a clear sign to them of their destruction, but of your salvation, and that from God."*

When you stand firm in your faith in Christ Jesus and do not become frightened of anything that opposes you, you will send a clear sign to your enemies of their destruction. This means that, when you stand firm in Christ, you are discouraging those who challenge your destiny. You are making your victories clear to the enemy and proving that you are a conqueror.

Standing firm in Christ produces good results in everything you do and qualifies you to be highly regarded by the Lord. Let not desperation, pressure from the enemy, desire for riches, exhaustion, faintness, weakness, stagnation, or doubt lead you to a state that will cause you to compromise your salvation. Your salvation cannot be bought at a price by any man. It is only through the Lord Jesus's blood that you were saved.

Matthew 26:69–75: *"Now Peter was sitting outside in the courtyard. And a servant girl came up to him and said, 'You also were with Jesus the Galilean.' But he denied it before them all, saying, 'I do not know what you mean.' And when he went out to the entrance, another servant girl saw him, and she said to the bystanders, 'This man was with Jesus of Nazareth.' And again he denied it with an oath: 'I do not know the man.' After a little while the bystanders came up and said to Peter, 'Certainly you too are one of them, for your accent betrays you.' Then he began to invoke a curse on himself and to swear, 'I do not know the man.' And immediately the rooster crowed. And Peter remembered the saying of Jesus, 'before the rooster crows, you will deny me three times.' And he went out and wept bitterly."*

Peter denied Jesus Christ three different times in three different ways. The first time, he merely denied. The second time his denial was coupled with an oath. The third time, he did not only deny with an oath, but he invoked a high-powered curse on himself. The more he denied Jesus, the more his sins were inflated to a higher degree. His third denial of Jesus was more vicious than the first denial. This means that any sin you continually do, consciously or unconsciously, invokes a greater evil over your life, and you lose the hope that was set for you in Christ Jesus. Peter sold himself in public in the midst of everyone. If it had not been for the prayer that Jesus offered for him before Peter denied Him, his soul could have remained in the hands of the devil. Only Jesus Himself could withstand that dreadful day when evil forces rose to oppose the sons of God. No man qualified to stand up against the evil that prevailed that day, and Peter's weakness was displayed openly for every man to see. He cried bitterly when he remembered what the Lord Jesus had said to him before his denial. His denial was followed by a fierce regret. His regret, his bitter cry, and his separation from his accusers made way for him to be accepted back into the kingdom of the Lord. Peter claimed his soul back. He claimed his integrity and his stand back into God's kingdom.

This should be your attitude when you know that you have publicly or secretly denied the Lord through your negative confessions or through refusing to become an ambassador of Christ Jesus when it mattered most. Regain your strength in God's kingdom and separate yourself from those you sold yourself to. Separate yourself from the company of evil and from those who caused you to lose your relationship with the Lord. Regret your deeds and remember the words of the Lord that you once heard from Him. Believe the promises He has for you in order to establish you to your rightful destination. Cry out to Him and reclaim your position, and He will restore you just as He restored Peter. Your dignity and your integrity cannot be compared with anything. They are a hedge that casts away evil intent. They are like a pillar that holds firm the high places, and they attract honor and glory to the most high God. First John 5:3: *"And his commandments are not burdensome."*

To keep God's command is not a burden, and to wait on Him is not folly. Allow the Lord to work His way into your life and stand firm, for He knows the right time for your breakthrough. He orchestrates the season for your miracle, and He understands how to open channels that will prosper you.

Performing Evil Rituals

Genesis 37:31: *"Then they took Joseph's robe and slaughtered a goat and dipped the robe in the blood."*

Slaughtering a goat is one of the ritual practices that some people perform as a sacrifice in order to attain wealth and protection. These practices are usually performed by individuals who believe that it is through the blood of a goat that a person's life can be redeemed from the spells pronounced to hinder his or her destiny.

Genesis 37:32: *"And they sent the robe of many colors and brought it to their father and said, "This we have found; please identify whether it is your son's robe or not.""*

Joseph's brothers knew that they had not ended his life, but because they wanted him dead, they were quick to tell their father that a fierce animal had killed him. Joseph's brothers were the ones who dipped his robe in the blood of a goat and went out to deceive their father. Their plan was one of the most wicked of acts in the book of Genesis. Jacob cried bitterly when he heard what had happened to his son. He was deeply sorrowful and distraught. This caused him to question the promises the Lord had for him and his sons. To Joseph's brothers it was just an act, but to Joseph's father it was a battle between himself and God. Jacob struggled to comprehend how God could have allowed his favorite son, Joseph, to be killed in the wilderness. Joseph's brothers used the blood of a goat in a malicious act to deceive and lie to their father, Jacob. Many people today perform and believe in such rituals—dipping other people's belongings in the blood of a goat—to cast away misfortune, curses, and spells.

Paula A. Price, PhD, in her book, *The Prophet's Dictionary: The Ultimate Guide to Supernatural Wisdom*,[1] defines a goat as a destructive presence that appears in prophetic circumstances. It signifies cruelty, brutality, perversity and the sinnal. If the slaughtering and the sacrifice of a goat in rituals signify such wicked attributes, how can you then resolve your troubles in life with it? A sacrifice will bring forth more bondage over your life. The blood will be used to hinder the genuine success the Lord has set aside for you. What the devil is doing to you through that goat is cruel and brutal. His intention is to slaughter your destiny just as you have slaughtered that goat. In life there is only one permissible way for you to accomplish your vision and to bring forth your dreams, and that is to immerse yourself and all that you have, by faith, in the blood of Jesus.

Hebrews 10:4 *"for it is impossible for the blood of bulls and goats to take away sins."* There is only one way of acquiring a destiny that is of the Lord, and that is sin-free living.

Some people are prosperous in life, and they are able to bless the poor and donate to charity. There is nothing wrong in donating your substance to charity and to the poor, but when what you have acquired has come through sacrificial blood of goats and animals, then all that you have is in vain. Just like Joseph's brothers deceived Jacob, you are being deceived. Your happiness will last for a moment, and your pleasures of life will all perish with you. At the end of everything, that sacrifice will cause you to cry when you see how the devil has clouded your life with deceit. Therefore,

---

[1]   Price, Paula A., PhD, *The Prophet's Dictionary: The Ultimate Guide to Supernatural Wisdom* (New Kensington, Pennsylvania, Whitaker House, 2006).

there is no need for you to acquire wealth through rituals and sacrifices of cattle and goats or by plotting for other people to perish so that you succeed.

Hebrews 10:5: *"Consequently, when Christ came into the world, he said, 'Sacrifices and offerings you have not desired, but a body have you prepared for me; in burnt offerings and sin offerings you have taken no pleasure. Then I said, "Behold, I have come to do your will, O God, as it is written of me in the scroll of the book.""'*

When your time of prosperity comes and your days of glory have arrived, you should speak like the Apostle Paul and proclaim these words, *"Behold, I have come to do your will, O God, as it is written of me in the scroll of the book."* For it is the sacrifice of Christ that has been offered for you to succeed. What is written about Christ being a sacrifice means that no other sacrifice is accepted if Christ Himself is rejected, for God does not take pleasure in any other sacrifice besides Him.

Matthew 15:6: *"For the sake of your tradition you have made void the word of God."*

Tradition should not by any means take the place of the word of God. If tradition is set aside, and we put our focus more on the word of God as our tradition, its effectiveness will be evident, and its power will also be visible in our lives. It is through the power of the word that you access the knowledge that leads to your destiny, rather than through ancient knowledge that produces carnality and failure. Any sacrifice you want to make should be offered through the conviction of the Holy Spirit. It is the Holy Spirit who will direct and guide you to your divine acceptable offering. The blood of Jesus cannot by any means be substituted by the blood of any man or animal. His blood purifies; it does not defile. On the contrary, the blood of animals defiles and does not purify.

Romans 12:1: *"I appeal to you therefore, brothers, by the mercies of God, to present your bodies as a living sacrifice, holy and acceptable to God, which is your spiritual worship. Do not be conformed to this world, but be transformed by the renewal of your mind, that by testing you may discern what is the will of God, what is good and acceptable and perfect."*

If you are aiming at doing the will of the Lord, conforming to the standards and practices of this world will not be a pleasant thing for you to do. What are those standards and practices?

Matthew 21:12–13: *"And Jesus entered the temple and drove out all who sold and bought in the temple, and he overturned the tables of the money-changers and the seats of those who sold pigeons. He said to them, 'It is written, "My house shall be called a house of prayer," but you made it a den of robbers.'"*

These people were bringing the standards of the world into the temple of the Lord. It is in the world where we sell and buy. But in God's kingdom you are freely given; there is nothing that you buy, and nothing will be sold for you. Success is not attached to any amount of money; you receive all things through Christ, the sacrifice offered for you.

Matthew 10:8: *"You received without paying; give without pay."*

There is no fee that can be attached to the grace that our Lord Jesus Christ has given for us. Freely He gives. Your healing is free, and you achieve every heart's desire without any fee.

It is not necessary for you to conform to worldly practices in order for you to make it in life. Therefore, there is no need for you to sell your integrity to get a business; meanwhile you could have attained a better offer when you could have kept your integrity. The key to a greater door lies in maintaining your integrity in times of desperation. Pursue righteousness, for in it there lies integrity, the weapon that silences all disputes of a righteous man.

These tables that Jesus found in the temple represent stable structures of immorality and lawlessness constructed by the enemy over your lifetime, which become the platform on which the devil may gamble. This gambling takes place on those who don't know who they are. But the Bible says Jesus came and overturned those stable structures in the temple. This is what

Christ does when you call unto Him; He comes to overturn wicked pillars raised to sustain evil patterns against your life.

The moment you begin to have a continual and intimate relationship with the Lord through prayer, know that your victories over principalities, worldly standards, and evil practices is certain.

Romans 11:11–12: *"So I ask, did they stumble in order that they might fall? By no means! Rather through their trespass salvation has come to the Gentiles, so as to make Israel jealous. Now if their trespass means riches for the world, and if their failure means riches for the Gentiles, how much more will their full inclusion mean!"*

Because of the trespasses of the Israelites, God transferred their riches to the Gentiles. The wealth that the Lord had prepared for the Israelites was taken over to the world. And what was meant for the world ended up in the hands of the Israelites. Many unbelievers are rich today because the people who are supposed to become the light of the world—believers—are themselves living in darkness, and hence their riches are seen in the hands of sinners. An exchange was done by the enemy over God's children, because they trespassed on God's law. To trespass means to enter or occupy something without permission. This intensely means that God's children do not adhere to the duties given to them by their master; rather, they comply with the activities of the kingdom of darkness. If you are a believer, your works should be pleasing before the Lord without any form of blemish. And if you are found having worldly practices that do not please the Lord, then your riches will be enjoyed by others. This raises jealousy in the hearts of God's children—the very same people destined to live a life of royalty.

Sometimes the people you minister salvation to receive it with an open heart and began to run with it whilst you don't believe in its power yourself. This brings about jealousy in the house of the Lord. Unbelief of a child of the Lord toward His power is transgression itself. It is very important for a person to receive the Lord's salvation and fully commit himself or herself to its principles in order to acquire the full measure of God's blessing in life. Most people today want to live like the rest of the world while they are saved; they forget that they are offering their riches to the world and in the process forfeiting spiritual gifts and fellowship with the Lord Himself. But those who truly seek the face of the Lord will not forfeit their treasures. They will not lose what God has prepared for them. They will live in palaces, and they will inherit the blessings of the Lord. Have purpose in your heart. Be righteous. Never live your life in disobedience to God's word, because blessings are awaiting those who persistently live according to His commands. The Lord is calling you to a righteous and holy life. God will not lie about fulfilling the promises He made concerning your life. Many may have been robbed by tradition and rituals, assuming they are on the right track with Jesus, but little did they know that they were exchanging the treasures for thistles and thorns. Some came in the name of the Lord to deceive God's children by leading them into evil practices and robbing them of their belongings. This is what the Lord is saying concerning those who have stolen from you.

Isaiah 33:1: *"Our enemies are doomed! They have robbed and betrayed, although no one has robbed them or betrayed them. But their time to rob and betray will end, and they themselves will become victims of robbery and treachery"* (Good News Translation).

Isaiah 33:10–15: *"'Now I will arise,' says the Lord, 'now I will lift myself up; now I will be exalted. You conceive chaff; you give birth to stubble; your breath is a fire that will consume you. And the peoples will be as if burned to lime, like thorns cut down, that are burned in the fire.' Hear, you who are far off, what I have done; and you who are near, acknowledge my might."*

Witches and evil ministers of the word are doomed, they robbed you in secret, but the Lord is announcing your reward to the nations. Your case is not a matter of secrecy anymore. The nation will know the power of the Lord through your life. God is saying that He has not acted until He begins to act for you and your family. This means that God will use His power, which many never knew existed, to act against those who robbed you. If you are a victim of robbery and treachery, the Lord is telling you that this is your season to see His power. He will use your case to silence your enemies. After He has completed His task, the only evidence of

His vengeance on your behalf will be ashes, and your victory will be pronounced to the nations. To those for whom the Lord will act, your case is next in line. Prepare yourself for a divine takeover, and when the Lord is finished, your foundations will be rebuilt with precious stones.

Isaiah 54:11: *"Behold, I will set your stones in antimony, and lay your foundations with sapphires."*

The Lord is destroying old foundations and laying out newer and stronger ones. Evil practices will no longer take their course over your life. Sapphire stones are commonly used to make jewelry. If stones of royalty are used by the Lord to lay out your foundations, what more will He use to decorate what He built? If it is your integrity the Lord is rebuilding, its foundations will not be done haphazardly. If it is your faith or your love toward Him that He is rebuilding, the Lord will use only precious building materials. From there afterward the Lord will decorate your life with more precious stones. This means that your prosperity relies on the foundation laid by the Lord. Your wealth and your riches are all the product of the Lord's foundations over your life.

Confusion in the Family

Genesis 37:35: *"All his sons and all his daughters rose up to comfort him, but he [Jacob] refused to be comforted and said, 'No, I shall go down to Sheol to my son, mourning.'"*

Jacob's response toward his family showed that he had given up on the promises of the Lord and the purpose for living. This was due to lies and deceit by his sons. He lost hope for living because his sons had reported to him that his favorite son had been killed by a fierce beast. This was nothing but lies. Genesis 37:29: *"When Reuben returned to the pit and saw that Joseph was not in the pit, he tore his clothes and returned to his brothers and said, 'The boy is gone.'"*

Reuben knew that Joseph was not where they had left him, in the pit, but they gave their father a false report that led to commotion in the family.

His sons had opened a door for the enemy to operate; Jacob's family was now under attack. The love of the Lord must be experienced in a family, and if we want to create a channel that would make an impact on others, we need to fix our own homes first.

Families are supposed to go to sacred places where God delights in their praise. And a total surrender of all members of the family presents them as a whole, in the manner in which the Lord placed each and every one of them to serve. What the Lord wants to do in your life is to arrange and put into place your family first, before you reach your greatest heights in life. A family forms a foundation of the calling of each and every believer, and it is an elevator to your greatness. It also forms a strong pillar upon which you should lean. The devil, knowing this, makes it very difficult for families to work together; Jacob's family is a good example. It was very difficult for Jacob to direct his family as the Lord wanted, because his sons themselves were pulling in different directions.

Jacob's family was a great family itself. The names of his sons were used to name the twelve tribes of Israel, and Jacob himself was a servant of the Lord. It is in such families of greatness that there exists a lot of tension and turmoil amongst members. The devil does not grant such kinds of families, peace. His aim is to weaken the visionary and abort the vision by bringing continuous conflict and dispute amongst the members of the family in an attempt to scatter them, continually attacking each one of them in their corners.

Matthew 10:34–36: *"Do not think that I have come to bring peace to the earth. I have not come to bring peace, but a sword. For I have come to set a man against his father, and a daughter against her mother, and a daughter-in-law against her mother-in-law. And a person's enemies will be those of his own household."*

One might ask, is Jesus not the prince of peace? (Isaiah 9:6). The one who said, *"Love your neighbor as yourself"* (Mark 12:31). The one who said, *"Before you offer anything on the altar make sure that you are in peace with everyone"* (Matthew 5:23–24). Absolutely, He is. Jesus is the Prince of Peace, and the foundation of His ministry is based on the peace He preached. Why is He coming with a sword, especially to families, to set a man against his father and a daughter against her mother?

Some believers misinterpret what the Lord Jesus Christ was implying concerning relationships amongst members of the family. They purposefully breakdown their homes claiming that Jesus did not come to bring peace on earth, but a sword. These words were not spoken out in favor of warfare, but out of love, to rebuke those who would deny Him within households. They are words spoken to encourage families to follow only Jesus and to believe in Him. The separation between father and son comes when either one of them rejects Jesus … where one is a believer and the other is an unbeliever. But it is His desire to see all members of the family following Him and living in harmony.

Jesus said to His disciples as He was sending them to minister unto people, *"Whatever house you enter, first say, 'Peace be to this house!' And if a son of peace is there, your peace will rest upon him. But if not, it will return to you. And remain in the same house, eating and drinking what they provide, for the laborer deserves his wages. Do not go from house to house"* (Luke 10:5–7).

The peace of the Lord in a family is a very important aspect in the Kingdom of the Lord. This is recognized by the teachings He gave His disciples as He sent them into villages. The first important thing the disciples did was to declare peace to the house before they could do anything else. The reason that peace is important is the fact that God dwells in it. Luke 10:6: *"And if the son of peace is there, your peace will rest upon him."*

A disciple should be a man of peace so that his peace can rest on the peace found in the house. That peace found in the house is Jesus Himself. This means that Jesus was already there in that house before the disciples arrived. The peace of Christ that prevailed in that home stood out to be the evidence of the presence of Jesus among the family members. If all members of the house are truly committed to Jesus, that house will be a house of peace. And the peace of the man of God on his arrival to that house activates an atmosphere conducive to the operation of disciples from that house to the rest of the village. That is why Jesus said, *"Remain in that same house … Do not go from house to house"* (Luke 10:7).

That house would become a centre of power for a disciple, because of the peace that was found in it. As a disciple, the glory of the Lord should forever be with you as you minister His word, and therefore you need the presence of the Lord to function all the time. This is what makes a peaceful home.

The sons and daughters who quarreled with their fathers and mothers began to have different mind-sets about the truth of what Jesus meant. God has placed you in that family for a reason. Your brightness should contaminate those you live with. Your zeal toward serving God should be noticed, and that alone should settle any dispute raised against you, because God Himself will not by any means allow shame to fall on you. It is your responsibility to usher your family to Christ and not allow division to prevail by misinterpreting the words spoken by our Lord concerning our relationships with those we should stand for. Good ambassadorship of Christ begins at home. Allow the glory of the Lord to be activated in your family through you.

Joshua 2:1: *"And Joshua the son of Nun sent two men secretly from Shittim as spies, saying, 'Go, view the land, especially Jericho.' And they went and came into the house of a prostitute whose name was Rahab and lodged there."*

Joshua 2:8: *"Before the men lay down, she came up to them on the roof and said to the men, 'I know that the Lord has given you the land, and that the fear of you has fallen upon us, and that all the inhabitants of the land melt away before you. For we have heard how the Lord dried up the water of the Red Sea before you when you came out of Egypt, and what you did at the two kings of the Amorites.'"*

Joshua 2:12–13 *"Now then, please swear to me by the Lord that, as I have dealt kindly with you, you also will deal kindly with my father's house, and give me a sure sign that you will save alive my father and mother, my brothers and sisters, and all who belong to them, and deliver our lives from death."*

If a prostitute wanted her family to be saved when the men of God lodged at her house what more could a believer, filled with spirit of God, having accepted Jesus as his or her personal savior, do besides stand in the gap for his father and mother, brothers and sisters. It is the desire of the Lord to save your family. All believers are strategically positioned by God in their households to impart the light. Conflicts should not be entertained; the Lord has not brought a sword among any members of your family. It is your approach that determines the wrath of the Lord against your loved ones. Because of Rahab, her household was saved, and those who mocked her perished.

Joshua 6:22–24: *"But to the two men who had spied out the land, Joshua said, 'Go into the prostitute's house and bring out from there the woman and all who belong to her, as you swore to her.' So the young men who had been spies went in and brought out Rahab and her father and mother and brothers and all who belonged to her. And they brought all her relatives and put them outside the camp of Israel. And they burned the city with fire, and everything in it."*

Joshua 6:25: *"But Rahab the prostitute and her father's household and all who belonged to her, Joshua saved alive."*

Rahab became an Israelite because she lodged the spies in her house. It was for the love she had for her family. She had an opportunity to rescue her life alone, but she thought of the destruction that would fall upon them if she did not take care of them. Even if her parents did not like the work that she was doing, she set that aside and negotiated a better life for them. Even if her family members told her that she was a disgrace to them, she set that aside and negotiated a new inheritance for them. The same work they mocked created a living for them as the children of the most high. It was Rahab's approach that delivered her household.

People might despise what you do, but if you have a good heart, you create a good platform from which God can transform your life. It is your mentality that determines the outcome of a matter. A bad circumstance can produce good results and a good circumstance can produce a bad result. It is all determined by your approach. Allow family dilemmas to have a good ending in which all members of the family will one day say that, if it had not been for you, they could have perished … they could all have gone astray. Let the story of your family begin by people mentioning the sacrifices and the contributions you have made for them, and when all that is accomplished, you can take on the entire globe. The world awaits people who begin their excellence by impacting the environment in which they were raised before they tackle issues of other families or groups.

In Wrong Authorities

Genesis 37:36: *"Meanwhile the Midianites had sold him in Egypt to Potiphar, an officer of Pharaoh, the captain of the guard."*

Most people believe that, just as Joseph became an important person in Egypt, so anyone qualifies to make it when in bondage or when in foreign nation. Some relate to what Joseph went through as if he knew that he was going to be sold into slavery in Egypt. Not every slave was sold; some were strangled or put in isolation for the rest of their captivity because they did not satisfy the set requirements and could not be sold. Joseph's situation was a unique one. And because of its uniqueness, he himself was supposed to be unique. Not everyone survives what Joseph went through. He experienced severe challenges before entering Egypt. It was his godly attributes that sustained him, and one such attribute, besides his faith, was that he was a pure hearted man; in other words, he had a good heart toward others. Imagine a man who does not have a good or pure heart leading a department in a foreign nation. He would definitely not make a great impact as Joseph did.

Joseph found himself in the hands of the wrong authorities in Egypt. Pharaoh saw him as a slave, not as a deliverer. He was captive; he was not free. He was a no-body, and this is where some people are. They find themselves in places where they are not appreciated, working for people who use their strength without any compliment or reward. They work tirelessly to produce what is best, but their efforts are wasted. When you find yourself in such an environment, know that you are in a similar situation to Joseph's when he found himself under the control of the wrong authorities in Egypt. This is where the differences between people come in. For the mere fact that you are in captivity does not mean God will deliver you. And because you are living far away from home does not make you a ruler. But it is when you purpose in your heart to do well under all unpleasant circumstances that you take on a unique identity. It is the loyalty and faithfulness toward man and God that set you aside for greatness.

Genesis 38:6–7: *"And Judah took a wife for Er his firstborn, and her name was Tamar. But Er, Judah's firstborn, was wicked in the sight of the Lord, and the Lord put him to death."*

Genesis 38:12–18: *"In the course of time the wife of Judah, Shua's daughter, died. When Judah was comforted, he went up to Timnah to his sheepshearers, he and his friend Hirah the Adullamite. And when Tamar was told, 'Your father-in-law is going up to Timnah to shear his sheep,' she took off her widow's garments and covered herself with a veil, wrapping herself up, and sat at the entrance to Enaim, which is on the road to Timnah. For she saw that Shelah was grown up, and she had not been given to him in marriage. When Judah saw her, he thought she was a prostitute, for she had covered her face. He turned to her at the roadside and said, 'Come, let me come in to you,' for he did not know that she was his daughter-in-law. She said, 'What will you give me, that you may come in to me?' He answered, 'I will send you a young goat from the flock.' And she said, 'If you give me a pledge, until you send it—'He said, 'What pledge shall I give you?' She replied, 'Your signet and your cord and your staff that is in your hand.' So he gave them to her and went in to her, and she conceived by him."*

Genesis 38:24–26: *"About three months later Judah was told, 'Tamar your daughter-in-law has been immoral. Moreover, she is pregnant by immorality.' And Judah said, 'Bring her out, and let her be burned.' As she was being brought out, she sent word to her father-in-law, 'By the man to whom these belong, I am pregnant.' And she said, 'Please identify whose these are, the signet and the cord and the staff.' Then Judah identified them and said, 'She is more righteous than I.'"*

When Tamar was brought before Judah, he did not give her a chance to tell her side of the story concerning her immorality. Judah was a man of authority when he went into Tamar, his daughter-in-law, and he had the final say. Wrong authorities are those who seek the distraction of others while they partake themselves of whatever they want. If you are under such leadership, it is only wisdom you need to possess. These are the conditions you should prepare for when you discover that you are governed by such people. Because of Tamar's immorality, Judah was prepared to burn her, publicly pronouncing how disappointed he was toward his daughter-in-law. The nation came to a standstill when they heard of the rigid sentence by Judah over Tamar. But little did he know that this time around his own misconduct would be at the centre stage. He was the father of the unborn child. Tamar knew the kind of person she was dealing with. That is why she had confiscated his signet, his cord, and his staff. The signet was Judah's emblem, the cord was his tie, and the staff was his stick, which signified his support. All of these made up the identity of a man of Judah's caliber. He never hesitated to agree to the defense brought about by Tamar simply because of the evidence that confirmed his identity as part of the indiscretion. If you know the kind of people who are leading you, acquire skills of defense as proof so you can set yourself free from any further public embarrassment. The point is, the destiny of most people is ended by those who are in authority, whether at work or at church, and it is your responsibility to strategically gather defense for times of accusation. It was Tamar's exaggerated efforts that exposed the hidden side of Judah—a side that many never knew existed, especially with regard to a man who was in the forefront of the law.

Are you one of those who are accused publicly by those who practice the same offence you committed? The Lord says, *"I have created the smith who blows the fire of coals and produces a weapon for its purpose. I have also created the ravager to destroy"* (Isaiah 54:16).

The Lord is the one who created the weapons that are intended to strike you. He is there in secret when your name is discussed by those who intend to bring you shame. Even if the army is rising up against you, the Lord has formed each and every one of those soldiers in that army. He has created their weapons and even the building where those weapons are made. Fear not! And may the Lord give you wisdom just like He gave Tamar to prevent your name from being publicly shamed by those occupying high seats.

Joseph was a faithful man; he had a pure heart and had a spirit of wisdom. These attributes gave him favor before Pharaoh, because the Lord favored him. And these are the attributes you should possess when you are in captivity. They are weapons that you should use to defend yourself when you are captive. They are suitable for fighting against conspiracies, evil schemes, and plots raised by the enemy to silence your voice and to prevent you from taking your next step.

Isaiah 54:17: *"You will have an answer for all who accuse you"* (Good News Translation).

If Tamar had not been wise, she could have been killed by her accusers; her future would have been terminated. Similarly, if Joseph had not been reliable, he could have died at the hand of Pharaoh. But because they had answers for those who accused them, they survived. Their answers were not given in words, but in actions against their accusers. And when they were justified, they did not seek revenge. They continued with life as if their lives had never been in danger. They forgot that the people around them once held their lives on a thread. Revenge raises new sets of enemies. When you seek revenge, it is not everyone who will be on your side, even if everyone was against you when you were in captivity.

Daniel 5:23: *"The God in whose hand is your breath, and whose are all your ways …"*

Your breath and your ways are in the hands of the Lord. There is nothing that can snatch you from Him. Your ups and downs take place in the hands of the Lord.

Mathew 23:1–4: *"Then Jesus said to the crowds and to his disciples, 'The scribes and the Pharisees sit on Moses' seat, so practice and observe whatever they tell you—but not what they do. For they preach, but do not practice. They tie up heavy burdens, hard to bear, and lay them on people's shoulders, but they themselves are not willing to move them with their finger.'"*

Christ is aware of the heavy burdens that you are made to carry by your authorities. It might be at work or anywhere else. It is the mission of the devil to demoralize you and prevent you from moving a step further. It does not matter that no one is backing your ideas or your vision; He will still see you through. It does not matter what sort of circumstance you find yourself in; He is constantly watching over you every step of the way. He is aware that the burdens are hard for you to bear. Carry that heavy burden, for the time will come when those who were carrying heavy burdens will carry nothing, and those who were carrying nothing will carry heavy burdens.

Luke 16:25: *"But Abraham said, 'Child, remember that you in your lifetime you received your good things, and Lazarus in like manner bad things.'"*

If Abraham reminded the rich man of the good things he had in his lifetime, don't think that the Lord is not seeing you today. He is not blindfolded; he can see very well the load you carry. He can see that nothing is working out for you. He can see that people have denied you what you deserve to possess. He can see that you are in bondage, and the devil is taking his turn with you. That load was not meant for you; it is the work of man that you are still struggling with today. No matter what is on your shoulders, bear it and bear it well, for the time is coming when you will be at the top. Wait patiently!

Habakkuk 2:2–3: *"And the Lord answered me: 'Write the vision; make it plain on tablets, so he may run who read it. For still the vision awaits its appointed time; it hastens to the end—it will not lie. If it seems slow, wait for it; it will surely come; it will not delay.'"*

The Lord is now calling on you to start running toward the destiny that He has prepared for you. He is telling you to run, despite the burden, and if your vision is delayed, wait for it. Wait! If your ministerial gifts seem slow to surface, keep on waiting for them patiently. One thing that assures you that you carry godly attributes is the extent of your patience toward God's affairs—the attitude you portray while waiting. It takes only a spiritual man to wait for his encounter with the Lord to yield spiritual gifts. To wait does not mean to cease or break up with your initial intent; rather, it means to hold on to the promises of the Lord concerning your life, and keep your vision to succeed alive at all time. You should always keep on believing and move swiftly to serve God without being too weary to do good to others. Wait, for your vision awaits its appointed time. In time you will become the focus of heaven, and you will gain the attention of the world. The people you see moving with the Spirit today also waited at some point in their lives. They had to endure their hardships, which you don't see at the moment, and the fact is, they waited. Do not despair, for your tomorrow is also waiting for you.

At the appointed time, Tamar received her twins instead of the shame that Judah had organized for her. Judah became disappointed when his plan to execute her did not succeed. This will be the outcome of your enemies who seek your downfall. They shall be disappointed, and their plans to put you to shame will fall on them instead. They shall accuse you in public with the intent to disgrace you only to realize that it is they who will instead become public disgraces. Sometimes in institutions people are called by their supervisors to be disgraced before everyone, but to the supervisors" amazement, the disgrace ends up turning on them. This was the case with Tamar and Judah. It is through that public disgrace that many did not find their way back into a position of well-being, and so they lost their destiny. Joseph also found favor in the sight of the Lord, and the appointed time came for him to rule. The appointed time is for those who are able to wait on the Lord despite the nature of their surroundings. It is for those who forgive openheartedly ... those who intend to keep their vision in prison. The Lord is turning your life around as well. You will experience a great uplift just when you are on the verge of being terminated by your superiors. They will not be able to prevent your elevation, and you will no longer be suppressed, because your light will become brighter than before. The Lord will have released you from their prison, and your finances and every blessing will be released from the cages of evil. Whatever cage is holding what belongs to you shall release what is yours. Your promotion will be taken from the hands of authorities and officials who have kept what the Lord has granted you. You will no longer be a prisoner to failure, oppression, depression, accusations, fear, doubt, immorality, sickness, limitation, curses, and stagnation. The Lord will terminate every conspiracy raised against your success preventing you to thrive. He is telling you to enter into your freedom today. Enter into your uplifting existence with the increase, multiplication, enlargement, prosperity, healing, and deliverance He has laid before you. Genesis 1:28: *"And God blessed them. And God said to them, 'be fruitful and multiply and fill the earth and subdue it and have dominion over the fish of the sea and over the birds of the heavens and over every living thing that moves on the earth.'"*

You are being restored to the original purpose you were created for—to be the captive He set free, to rule, to govern, and to be a person of authority. You are set free to govern your nation by occupying higher seats and to be a man or woman of authority in His kingdom by being a spear that pierces through evil, corruption, and wicked schemes. Your freedom will guarantee you topmost achievements in your career. Go on and glorify the Lord, for He has granted you victory before your accuser. His name is great, and so shall be yours.

Chapter 4

Subjected to Great Heat and Pressure

First John 5:4: *"For everyone who has been born of God overcomes the world. And this is the victory that has overcome the world—our faith."*

You must desire to be called the son or the daughter of the most high and allow Him to give birth to you, for by so doing you access your victory to overcome the things of this world. When challenges come, you will overcome; when shortcomings appear, you will never run short. In everything you do, you will overcome. It is like entering into a boxing ring to fight your opponent, and before the fight begins an announcement is made: "Ladies and gentlemen, this gallant opponent has defeated his opponent with a knockout in the first round!" Jesus made that announcement when He was on the cross. John 19:30: *"When Jesus had received the sour wine, he said, 'It is finished,' and he bowed his head and gave up his spirit."*

That was an announcement that our Lord Jesus Christ made at the cross on Calvary. It was as if He said, "My dear child, it is finished; you have overcome. It is finished; you are victorious, and everything you aspire to have you shall possess." The Lord has already made everything possible for you. The bow of Jesus on the cross was for those who believe that they have overcome their troubles on earth. It was a bow that signified a compliment to you that, despite what you see with your physical eyes, you managed to pull out from the rest and make an impact. Despite the great heat and pressures of life, you see yourself in the manner the Lord sees you.

Great Heat and Pressure

Proverbs 24:10: *"If you faint in the day of adversity, your strength is small."*

In a manufacturing company that produces clay bricks, the bricks are baked in a big furnace before they can be sold and used for erecting buildings. These clay bricks are all prepared the same way; they are identical, with the same mixture of chemical components, and only very slightly different in size and weight. They are fired in the furnace for the same length of time, and when they are packed, no one can identify one from another; they all look the same and have the same color. If they are kept for a longer time in the fire, however, they start to take different forms depending on their ability to withstand the heat. These bricks begin to take on a different form as they are produced through this process. Nothing tampers with them besides the furnace they remain in. Days pass by, and these bricks begin to take on different colors, and at the end of the process, the furnace is put out, and the bricks are sorted according to their similarities. The stronger bricks are packed together. The weaker bricks are packed together. And those that are average are also packed together. The color and texture usually determine the category of each brick. Depending on their beauty, strength, color, and texture, these bricks are classified and grouped together. This process produces up to six and more different brick types. Those that are not well baked are the cheapest bricks. They did not experience as much fire as those that are expensive. Some of those that have experienced fire for a longer time are smoother and stronger than those that did not. Cheaper bricks are easily breakable because they possess less strength, and they crumble when they experience adversity.

It may be easy for you to say you want to be like that expensive, beautiful brick that people would want to build with. But the truth of the matter is, it won't be easy for you to stay in the furnace and be baked.

First Corinthians 3:12–14: *"Now if anyone builds on the foundation with gold, silver, precious stones, wood, hay, straw—each one's work will become manifest, for the Day will disclose it, because it will be revealed by fire, and the fire will test what sort of work each one has done. If the work that anyone has built on the foundation survives, he will receive a reward."*

In your pursuit of greatness, it is very important for you to have a strong foundation in the word of God on which you can build everything. Unless the Lord puts you in the fire for a period of time, all you have will crumble because of the inferior material you used to build it. When God is busy in other people's lives, sometimes the moment they feel the heat; they jump out of the furnace. As a result, they become half-baked believers who can't make a progress in their spiritual journey. Pressures of life are a way of preparing you for greatness. The more the heat you absorb, the more beautiful and strong you will become, and the Lord will have no choice but to use you for special occasions, simply because you are an expensive brand. It is not a wise move for you to jump out of the furnace, because pressures from the Lord do not last forever. No man has ever inherited the blessing of the Lord peacefully without going first through the trials and tribulations of life. There has to be that particular area in any person's life that keeps on raising the temperature of the furnace. If it's not marriage it's work related, and if it's not work related, it has to do with your children. If it is not children, perhaps it is a chronic ailment of some sort. Some experience all manner of trials all at once and yet withstand the heat; ultimately, their reward becomes immense.

Plants and other living matter that lived millions of years ago died and withstood great heat and pressure. In that process, they turned into coal that produces energy to give us electricity. It all did not happen in a day. Allow the Lord to finish His work over your life.

Mark 15:33: *"And when the sixth hour had come, there was darkness over the whole land until the ninth hour. And at the ninth hour Jesus cried with a loud voice, 'Eloi, Eloi, lema sabachthani?' which means, 'My God, my God, why have you forsaken me?'"*

These are the words of Jesus when He was preparing Himself to come out of His furnace. When you notice that no one is close to you in times of trouble, and those you expected would help you are silent to your call, know that you are at the maximum level of your heat. And when you have stood your maximum level of heat, and all that you can say is "Why, Lord?" know that you have entered the pinnacle of your glory. Jesus did not jump off the cross when there was no response; instead, He stood. When darkness has covered you and there is no one for you to run to, do not jump off the cross, for your victory has come!

To ask the Lord "Why?" is not a sin, especially if you have been sure to your commitment to Him. It is your commitment to God that determines your utterances to Him. Most people will begin to wonder if you are truly a child of God just as they did when Jesus was hanged on the cross.

Romans 9:21–23: *"Has the potter no right over the clay, to make out of the same lump one vessel for honorable use and another for dishonorable use? What if God, desiring to show his wrath and to make known his power, has endured with much patience vessels of wrath prepared for destruction, in order to make known the riches of his glory for vessels of mercy, which he has prepared beforehand for glory."*

How do you want the Lord to use you? Do you want Him to use you as a vessel of honor, or do you want to become a vessel that brings dishonor? Some people want to do great things for the Lord, and their names will be written in the book of life in the section called "God's Heroes." If you want to fall under that category, then allow the potter to make what He wishes of you, don't resist Him by refusing to obey His word when you go through trials and pressures of life. Praise Him in all circumstances, and learn to love Him in all circumstances, for He is faithful and will never lead you astray. When you experience pressures of life, know that God is granting you the platform to become faithful, and to allow Him to create a vessel of honor out of your circumstances.

Firmly Rooted

Colossians 2:6–7: *"Therefore, as you received Christ Jesus the Lord, so walk in him, rooted and built up in him and established in the faith, just as you were taught, abounding in thanksgiving."*

Before you can be rooted in Christ, you must first live for Him. A seed lives for a moment of time in the soil before its roots can develop and begin to protrude deeper into the soil. It is your consistent life in Christ that will make it possible for you to be deeply rooted in Him. Having a lifestyle in Jesus Christ creates stronger roots for your existence. When you create these roots, your faith also becomes a lifestyle. This means that, before you make any decision concerning your life, you should think of the Lord first. If you do this, the Lord will download into your mind solutions you need to succeed. As a person who aspires to go into business, the ministry, or an academic career, build up your faith around Jesus Christ. The Bible says, *"Therefore, as you received Christ Jesus the Lord, so walk in him* (Colossians 2:6).

Walking in Jesus means that you exist inside of Him; He is the container in which you exist. Now, when you exist in such an environment, failure can never be your portion simply because of the environment you live in. When defeat intrudes the premises of your vision, the environment you live in will not be conducive for its manifestation. When you encounter fear to make it in life, your fears will vanish simply because of the environment in which you find yourself. There is no way the devil will be able to claim his way into your life. All of his schemes will not stand in your way to achieving what you want to achieve. All his plans will be cast far away from you. One may ask, why then am I going through troubles, fears, and failure when I am found in Christ Jesus? You have to understand this: when you are in Christ, you are not like the rest. The troubles you go through are elevations; they are designed to promote you. Jesus was a man of faith Himself, and He used the challenges He came across to elevate God's kingdom and to strengthen Himself in the Lord. This should be your attitude when you come across life's challenges when you are in Christ. When Jesus was ministering, there was only one goal that stood above the rest, and that was to uplift the faith of the people toward their Maker. There is nowhere in the Bible were Jesus commanded a person to rise and walk, for His holiness had healed him. In fact, Jesus did not preach holiness; rather, He preached repentance by faith, because He knew that in the process, faith in the Lord would bear holiness. Faith is the beginning factor that can instigate in you all the godly attributes you need to become effective.

Have a desire today to walk by faith, as this is what pleases God. Why is God pleased by faith? Because it is an act you take toward God in order for Him to give you a response. It is that extra step that you take when all solutions have failed. You can miss a holy man, but you can't miss a man of faith, because faith enables everyone to witness around you the rewards of your faith. Faith is a mode of communication between you and God.

Spiritual things are too complicated to be understood, especially with our carnal eyes. Save yourself some breath and just overflow with thanksgiving before God in desperate times. If you try to calculate whether it is God or the devil who has brought calamity into your life or why God allowed this or that to happen in your life, or you begin to point out those people who did not experience the hardships you encountered, you will be paving your way to what will not benefit you. All that will affect your faith, and it won't be possible for you to walk in Christ Jesus. When you are built up in Him, it is not necessary for you to understand some-things. All you must know is that, ultimately, you will become victorious, no matter the affliction. You are rooted in Christ, and this means that you are rooted in your solutions and in your direction. Is it wrong then when you are rooted in Christ to ask yourself questions when things don't go right? Absolutely not. But don't become hooked on questioning Him, as that will lead you to complain, and in the process you will compromise your faith, because you will then not see the possibility of coming out of your circumstances. Therefore, be firmly rooted in Christ and live in Him.

The Bible says walk in Christ. It does not say stay in Him. What's the difference, then, between walking in Christ and staying in Him? Now, physically walking is an exercise. This means that, when you walk in Christ, something is exercised, and that thing is your faith. This enables you to be active and lively. Imagine what would happen if you could stay in the Lord without doing anything. You would probably not exercise what the Lord has given to you that make Him aware that you acknowledge His existence and His role in your life. You walk by faith in all circumstances to overcome all life's difficulties. What does walking by faith mean? It means that you know deep in your heart that you will overcome all things through Christ Jesus no matter the challenges. Take a step to move away from that place of adversity. One step after another will make it possible for you to believe and walk in Him, because He will make sure that you are always strengthened so you can take another step. Walk in the Lord by believing that Christ has what it takes to give you a happy and joyful ending no matter the conditions you find yourself in.

Just Provide

Isaiah 55:10: *"For as the rain and the snow come down from heaven and do no return there but water the earth, making it bring forth and sprout, giving seed to the sower and bread to the eater."*

When God entrusts you with something, that thing is not for you alone; it is to share with those in need. There is a seed deposited in each and everyone of us, and it only takes the word of God to water the seed in order to bear fruits that many will feed on. Most people complain that they bless others, and meanwhile nothing is happening in their lives. They don't realize that God has given that gift to them so they can be a blessing to others. Our lives are supposed to bless others and not just satisfy ourselves.

You must allow the seed of the Lord to grow in you, and in return give out bread to the eater. If you look at it that way, you will be at peace with yourself when people you once assisted receive their elevation before you. Even biologically most animals and fruit trees do not feed on what they produce. Cows don't feed on meat and milk and fruit trees are only supplied with water and fertilizers so that they can produce fruit. Similarly your gifts are not only for you; they are for you to share with those who are around you; these are what we call the eaters. You are a seed-bearing person. You must grow so that people will come from all over to feed from your abundance.

Imagine what could have happened if Jesus had come on earth for Himself. Jesus came on earth to liberate us, because He was free Himself. His freedom was given to you. Similarly, your duty is to feed from the word and in the process be watered and be taken care of by the wine dresser who is your Maker. Look upon the Lord and share with others what you have, and carry your responsibility to serve others without complaining.

Second Corinthians 8:3–10: *"For they gave according to their means, as I can testify, and beyond their means, of their own accord, begging us earnestly for the favor of taking part in the relief of the saints—and this, not as we expected, but they gave themselves first to the Lord and then by the will of God to us. Accordingly, we urged Titus that as he had started, so he should complete among you this act of grace. But as you excel in everything—in faith, in speech, in knowledge, in all earnestness, and in our love for you—see that you excel in this act of grace also. I say this not as a command, but to prove by the earnestness of others that your love also is genuine. For you know the grace of our Lord Jesus Christ, that though he was rich, yet for your sake he became poor, so that you by his poverty might become rich. And in this matter I give my judgment: this benefits you."*

By feeding on the word, you allow the seed in you to germinate, and in the process you are giving yourself to the Lord. The Bible says, after you have given yourself to the Lord then by the will of God give yourself to others (Second Corinthians 8:5). This means that your possessions, time and assistance should be used to advance others. When you give yourself first to God and then to others, you are acting on the grace of God which Paul says, he wishes that Titus should complete among others that act of grace, for it is the will of the Lord (Second Corinthians 8:6). Paul is saying that, there are people who are waiting for you to assist them so that they may excel as you excel. That is the reason that the Lord is taking you to greater heights—so that you can pull others as well. The Lord is giving you that managerial post so that His grace may be seen in you, and so that others might also excel in their respective areas. The Lord will place in you companies worth millions so that you may elevate others. When you think of the needs of others before you think of your own needs, you are acting on genuine love, and God's love. That love represents His presence. Learn to give to others your last supply, your valuables, and anything you put in High esteem. This will become a gateway to your own uplifting.

Emptying yourself to others need is a sign of God's grace upon your life and in other people's lives as well. Christ became poor in order for us to be rich. In your riches of the word, and the knowledge of Him, you should always share His word totally, and wholly encourage the world in His truthfulness without sparing or limiting the knowledge of Christ that He richly blessed us with. Even with your earthly riches, wealth, and possessions, the act of showing and giving to others is very important before the Lord, because it signifies love and caring for others.

Luke 16:19–21: *"There was a rich man who was clothed in purple and fine linen and who feasted sumptuously every day. And at his gate was laid a poor man named Lazarus, covered with sores, who desired to be fed with what fell from the rich man's table."*

Are there people at your gates you are failing to provide for? Are you not concerned about what people you see each and every single day put in their stomachs or what their needs are? The Lord is taking you to a place where you will give without any reservations. You will give knowing that God will increase all that you have offered. You will give, and all that you gave you shall receive in duplicate and triplicate.

Just allow the grace of God to work over your life, as that will be an act of love. God in His abundance will make a way for you to give what He has given to you to the needy, both materially and spiritually. In you there is a tree of fruit that many will come to feed on. Your ideas will change your community. Your thinking will save the cry of the people in your village. Many will come from all over to receive the word … to receive solutions to their long-unresolved challenges. You will teach the statues of the Lord, you shall live your life in financial overflow, and you shall have plenty to share with others. Just allow yourself to become a channel of supply of God's resources to those who are in need and to those who need uplifting.

Do Not Stop Anywhere

Isaiah 31:1: *"Woe to those who go down to Egypt for help and rely on horses, who trust in chariots because they are many and in horsemen because they are very strong, but do not look to the Holy One of Israel or consult the Lord."*

There are times in life when people become desperate for solutions and find themselves in great need of better lives. There are also times in life when the Lord becomes silent, and there is no sign of any heavenly beings around. There are times when you have yelled and called to no one but to the Lord, and you feel as if your prayers are reaching the clouds. It is in such instances that many follow the masses and become associated with mighty men and their chariots. One mistake that you should not commit is to forsake your Lord and follow those you believe will bring an immediate solution to your problems.

Egypt is a place of great wisdom. It is full of immeasurable knowledge, and many depended on the Egyptians for defense and for consultation. It is a place that brings about brilliant ideas, and because of that some consider it wise to make a move to follow the ways of the Egyptians instead of the ways of God. When you are in such great need of an intervention in your downward life, you might see many offers of Egyptian mentality that will be very hard to resist. Consulting a spiritualist, seeking people's backup, devising quicker and easier ways to be uplifted, and forsaking the Lord are some of the ways in which you invite reproach from the Lord. You need to come to the understanding that God's silence is a weapon of the wise. When God is silent it does not mean He is sidelining you. God is how you see Him; He is a being you visualise in your spirit and soul when He seems not to be there when you are in need of Him. What does that mean? It means that God will become what you want Him to become. If you believe that He is not there when you pass through the fire, He will seem not to be there. But if you live like the wise and believe that God is everywhere and there is nothing hidden from Him and there is nothing difficult for Him to do, it is just a matter of time for His visitation to be evident. The art of waiting for the Lord is what most of us lack, and it is key to all of man's greatest opportunities.

Yes, to wait on the Lord is not an easy task. Additionally, no man will find it easy—indeed, it may be impossible—to close any of the doors the Lord has opened for you. Just when you think that you are completely exhausted, He is near with your answer, and you realize that you have not even begun to wait for Him. One secret that you should have when waiting on the Lord is that you should never look at how long you have waited.

The best time for you to calculate the time you spent waiting is when you appreciate Him after you have received what you have long waited for.

Genesis 19:15: *"As morning dawned, the angels urged Lot, saying, 'Up! Take your wife and your two daughters who are here, lest you be swept away in the punishment of the city.'"*

Genesis 19:16–17: *"And they brought him out and set him outside the city. And as they brought them out, one said, 'Escape for your life. Do not look back or stop anywhere in the valley. Escape to the hills, lest you be swept away.'"*

Lot was commanded by one of the angels not to look back to witness the punishment of Sodom and Gomorrah; neither was he to stop anywhere in the valley. This punishment was for the sins of men and women who had spoken evil against the will of the Lord. Lot was commanded to move from the valley to the hills. For us, this means that when we know that we have been set free or delivered, it becomes our responsibility to move from the valley to the hills. This becomes your responsibility. You must force yourself out of the crowd to a more convenient place. Lot was reluctant to come out of the corrupt and evil city; in fact, an angel had to hold him by the hand to help him make his way out. This shows how Lot was attached to the environment in which he found himself.

In most cases, we find it very complicated to come out of evil practices or evil surroundings. And even if we find mercy from the Lord, we still find it too difficult to come out of the places of destruction. An angel of the Lord had to pull Lot by the hand, because he did not realize the urgency of the Lord's message that he must go to the hills to avoid the terror.

Through experiences like this one, the Lord teaches us some of the fundamental principles of reaching the top in whatever endeavor you pursue. The first one is that: do not look back at any unpleasant situations that transpired in your life. When you have lost everything, do not look back at what you have lost. It may be your possessions, your career, your marriage, your finances, your loved ones, or even your vision. Whatever it maybe, the Lord is telling you not to look back. The second point is that you should not stop anywhere. In other words, when there is a particular position you are destined for, do not assume a resting mentality until you acquire that position. The place you choose for your little rest might end up being your final destination! Those who have enrolled for their studies and then have taken a break will testify to the fact that coming back to studying is very difficult. When you return to the learning institution, not only do you find yourself a stranger there, but many things have changed as well. If you are constantly applying for a new job and you have been receiving regret notices, and this causes you to give up and not send any more applications, that is a sign that you are discouraged. And you will realize that, the moment you begin to send applications again, you will find it difficult to believe that you will ever get a job. Keeping the momentum is what God is talking about. Looking forward is the best mechanism to survive the disappointments of the past. People who stay at their point of breakdown are swept away by the punishment of the Lord. Decide not to be Lot's wife, who disobeyed God, looked back, and turned into a pillar of salt! The mercy of the Lord is already available to help you reach your destiny. God has already sent an angel to take you by the hand to force you out of ashes to greener pastures. But there are things that you should do: carry yourself and keep on walking, facing forward without stopping anywhere in the valley. Depression, doubt, stagnation are all valleys. Take that step and move on.

Genesis 19:18–22: *"And Lot said to them, 'Oh, no, my lords. Behold, your servant has found favor in your sight, and you have shown me great kindness in saving my life. But I cannot escape to the hills, lest the disaster overtake me and I die. Behold, this city is near enough to flee to, and it is a little one. Let me escape there—is it not a little one?—and my life will be saved!' He said to him, 'Behold, I grant you this favor also, that I will not overthrow the city of which you have spoken. Escape there quickly, for I can do nothing till you arrive there.'"*

The Lord said, *"I can do nothing till you arrive there."* Even if Lot ultimately lived in the hills, the place the Lord had initially destined for him, he negotiated his way with the Lord to go to a nearby city, because he noticed that he was not going to make it in time to the hills, and the disaster would overtake him on the way. The point is, even if things were hard on him, he went back to the Lord and requested alternative means that would spare his life. Lot did not rely on other means besides the Lord. He did not decide to change the route without consulting the Lord. He understood that it was the Lord who had taken him out of destruction, and it was only the Lord who would enable him to reach the city safely. And the Lord granted his request. The mistake that some make, is that, they forsake the Lord—the very one who took them out of punishment and delivered them into liberty. They begin to use their discretion to seek out what they believe is what is right for them without involving the one who holds their direction. Just as He did with Lot, the Lord has shown you kindness, and He will continue to show you His favor in all that you do. It is not the traditional doctors who have shown you mercy, and it is not the might of the army that has spared your life. It is the Lord who redeems His own from destruction. Glorify His holy name; only He approves and permits the intention of man.

Becoming a Hearer and Doer of the Word

Daniel 3:15: *"Now if you are ready when you hear the sound of the horn, pipe, lyre, trigon, harp, bagpipe, and every kind of music, to fall down and worship the image that I have made, well and good."*

What sound are you hearing? Is it the sound of the Lord or the sound of evil? Is it the sound to do well or is it the sound to do evil? Is the sound that you are hearing leading you before the Lord or before the devil? When you hear a particular sound, do you abandon the ways of the Lord to worship evil? Understand that you don't need to see or touch the image in order to worship it. An image or a god is anything that you use as a substitute for the true God. Christians have never seen God before, but still they worship Him. The same thing is applicable when you worship the devil; you don't have to see him to worship him. When you substitute God's principles with something or somebody else's principles, you are worshiping an idol. Idolatry is anything that stands in the way of the worship of the true God.

Why do you think King Nebuchadnezzar made all instruments in his kingdom make a call for an idol worship? The thing is, the king wanted every instrument to sound and call forth all people to the worship of an image. Similarly, the devil still uses the same sounds of instruments to call forth people to worship him. The devil uses different kinds of music to lead people into cult worship. Even some gospel lyrics are links to a certain deity, which leads many to idolatry, and that is the case in some churches. You see, if you sing gospel music and you do not want to be born again, you are sentencing yourself to judgment. Gospel music is not a type of music you listen to for relaxation or because you feel a bit down; it is an act of worship to a God who is alive. This is singing with understanding and truth to usher His spirit into your life. Choose today to hear the type of sound that the Lord wants you to hear—the elementary sound you should always incline your ear to in order to shun evil.

Daniel 3:16–17: *"Shadrach, Meshach, and Abednego answered and said to the king, 'O Nebuchadnezzar, we have no need to answer you in this matter. If this be so, our God whom we serve is able to deliver us from the burning fiery furnace, and he will deliver us out of your hand, O king. But if not, be it known to you, O king, that we will not serve your gods or worship the golden image that you have set up.'"*

What does "serving an idol" mean to you? Does it mean you stand before the image and stare at it for a moment, leaving your traces behind? Definitely not. The moment you present yourself to an idol, you have pronounced yourself an idol worshiper. Whatever activity you do, even if you are away from the idol, will be linked to it, and your destiny will be dedicated to evil. This is what causes many to fail in life. All your actions and speeches will be exalting that god, and that prevents you from serving a true God. You cannot worship a false god for a moment and later on worship the living God. You cannot compromise God in the morning and worship Him in the evening. This secret was revealed to Shadrack, Meshack, and Abednego. The king asked them to only worship the image briefly, and after that they might continue with their daily routines, but to them it meant something else. To them it meant serving two images no matter where they were and no matter how long they knelt down before the image. To them, the split second they spent worshiping an image equaled an entire eternity denying God.

You don't have to work like a slave for a god before you become accepted as a true worshiper. Some have lost their destinies to the hands of the devil by accompanying a friend or a brother in the ways of evil. Honor the Lord with your works before man. Many believers have fallen victim of allowing the world to dictate to them how they should handle themselves. In your workplace, is Christ exalted or compromised? Is Christ the head, or is there an idol that wants you to bow down and worship when the siren rings? Some managers abuse and misuse their powers; they confuse God's place with their own.

Luke 8:19: *"Then his mother and his brothers came to him, but they could not reach him because of the crowd. And he was told, 'Your mother and your brothers are standing outside, desiring to see you.' But he answered them, 'My mother and my brothers are those who hear the word of God and do it.'"*

Jesus expected His mother and brothers to live by the word; not only that, He expected them to perform it. One question you should ask yourself is, why was it so difficult for Mary to see her son, Jesus? Now if Jesus expected His mother to be a person of the word, should you not expect the same of your supervisor? And your brothers? You should not compromise the word of God for anything, whether at work or at school or in your nation. Those who hear and do God's word are the ones you will find next to Jesus—not relatives.

The thing with the kingdom of God is that we sometimes wish that we could work with people that we feel comfortable with, but the truth of the matter is that people who should be close to us should be those who do God's will. Jesus set a simple yet complex precedent: let not those who do God's word suffer for the sake of relationships.

Jesus's brothers could not meet with Him because of the crowd that surrounded Him. Look at your life and inspect the crowds that are preventing you from hearing or doing the word of God. Is it a financial hindrance? Or are you crowded by doubt and unbelief? Or is poverty crowding your mind so you can't hear the word of the Lord? Are sickness and infirmities limiting you in your reach to Jesus? Do not allow anything to prevent you from looking forward to your Jesus. It does not matter how long you have been crowded by limitation and bondage caused by ignorance and idolatry. It is the Lord's desire to terminate that covenant and set you free. Now, promise in your heart to become a hearer and a doer of the word of God despite policies and rulings made by man. Stand your ground, resist evil, and Jesus will call you brother. So shall your soul and treasures be released from cages and prisons of the kingdom of darkness.

Chapter 5

Advanced Deceptions

Matthew 24:24: *"For false christs and false prophets will arise and perform great signs and wonders, so as to lead astray, if possible, even the elect."*

We are living in the days during which evil has risen against the elect of the Lord. Many have been led astray by those who claim to be servants of the most high. These agents of the kingdom of darkness perform the same miracles performed by the true servants of God. Even other true servants of God do not perform great signs compared to those of the false prophet. The term *false prophet* has dominated the minds of people more than the term *true prophet*—to such an extent that a true servant of the Lord can doubt another true servant of the Lord. Everyone is comfortable in his or her own corner because no one wants to risk his or her ministry by handing it over to one of the false prophets. This is how the devil has set apart servants of the Lord. At the mention of false prophets, everyone closes the door and does not want to become a victim of circumstance.

First Timothy 6:20–21: *"O Timothy, guard the deposit entrusted to you. Avoid the irreverent babble and contradictions of what is falsely called 'knowledge,' for by professing it some have swerved from the faith."*

What "knowledge" are you acquiring? Is it the knowledge of Christ or a false doctrine that has been deposited in your life by those who want to swerve you from the faith? In these last days, the devil will come for those who call themselves the faithful of Christ. He will bring to them doctrines that will sound convincing about our Lord Jesus Christ.

These may be true men of God who don't realize that they are falling into the intentions of the enemy, because Apostle Paul revealed that, in the last days, the devil is coming for those who call themselves faithful of Christ. Now the question is, what schemes will the devil use when he comes for the faithful of the Lord? Secondly, how can the devil overcome one who is faithful to his God? Well, the first and basic strategy he uses is to scare true men of God with the term *false prophet*. And when they hear that term, everyone goes back to his habitat. Paul is saying to Timothy, guard the deposit entrusted to you. Guarding the deposit means that Timothy should evaluate every small thing offered to him in speech, because Paul understood that it is through small talk that most believers open a door to be deceived by the enemy. You have to know that the devil is very strategically minded and very calculative. Therefore, if you don't guard the deposit entrusted to you he will snatch it. And because the faithful are guarding the deposit entrusted to them, he believes that to guard means to isolate, and this is where many are being deceived.

Following are terms echoed by the devil in the minds of the people in an attempt to deceive them in order to terminate what the Lord has intended about their lives.

"I am All Right"

Luke 21:34: *"But watch yourselves lest your heart be weighed down with dissipation and drunkenness and cares of this life."*

One of the deceptions the devil uses against some of God's children is to make them believe that, when they have received Christ as their personal savior, all is settled and there is no need for anything else; the good life has began. Nothing is settled until you act on your salvation and on the purpose you were called for.

The Bible says *"watch yourselves lest your heart be weighed down."* This means you should be on the lookout to make sure you are not deceived by the devil. You make sure you are always living a life that pleases God.

Most people get used to God and later miss the reason they were called into His kingdom.

It is very important for you to watch and guard your speech and all that is spoken into your life. The moment you begin to be comfortable and think that all is all right, know that you have given your soul and your destiny to the devil. The truth is, we will fight the devil until Christ comes.

Luke 8:22–24: *"One day he got into a boat with his disciples, and he said to them, 'Let us go across to the other side of the lake.' So they set out, and as they sailed he fell asleep. And a windstorm came down on the lake, and they were filling with water and were in danger. And they went and woke him, saying, 'Master, Master, we are perishing!'"*

If the storm had not come, the faith of His disciples would not have been tested. They were relaxed, comfortable, and everything was all right—until the storm came. And as the storm arose, no one was expecting it. This is how some people respond to disaster; they never think it will evercome. Always be on guard so that you may be ready to tackle each and every unexpected matter that comes your way. It is not all right until you guard your heart and all activities that happen around you. Disaster is there for you to prepare for and conquer.

To be on guard means to attack and prepare before the devil strikes, and by so doing you have secured a step toward your destiny. Cover your unborn children with the blood of Jesus. Pronounce and declare healing to all members of your family before they become sick. Proclaim riches and wealth before you receive any major project. Prophesy greatness over your life before anyone sees anything in you. When you continually declare God's word as a watchman, it is then you will be all right.

Jeremiah 6:16–17: *"Thus says the Lord: 'Stand by the roads, and look, and ask for the ancient paths, where the good way is; and walk in it, and find rest for your souls. But they said, "We will not walk in it." I set watchmen over you, saying, and "Pay attention to the sound of the trumpet!" But they said, "We will not pay attention."'"*

There is no way you will reach your destiny by refusing to seek guidance from those who have walked the paths you are on. The moment you fail to become a watchman, your steps to greatness will cease. Pay attention to the sound that calls your name to the nations.

Psalm 25:12: *"Who is the man who fears the Lord? Him will he instruct in the way that he should choose."*

In other words, the Lord will instruct you in the ways you want to pursue. This means that the fear of the Lord is key in assisting you to unlock the true ways on which you should walk. Many people are successful today. They live the life anyone would envy, but because they don't have the fear of the Lord in their spirit, their souls are in captivity. A true destiny begins with the fear of the Lord. Therefore nothing happens until you work out your salvation in fear of the Lord. Then the Lord will instruct you which way to choose. This means that you can choose what you want to become in life, and the Lord will simply instruct you how to get there. He will tell you what to do and what not to do. He will show you the relevant people you should work with, and He will guide each and every single step you take. Decide today what business you want to start, and the Lord will instruct you so you can attain it. Choose your destiny, and the Lord will choose your ways.

"This Sin Is Not So Bad"

Matthew 5:21–22: *"You have heard that it was said to those of old, 'You shall not murder; and whoever murders will be liable to judgment.' But I say to you that everyone who is angry with his brother will be liable to judgment; whoever insults his brother will be liable to the council; and whoever says, 'You fool!' will be liable to the hell of fire."*

We sometimes think that those who are susceptible to hellfire are those who have committed serious crimes and have been locked up in prison for a very long time. Jesus made a very intense statement about people who don't mind how they talk to others. He said, if you call someone a fool, you are *"liable to the hell of fire."* That means you are most likely to be there. This statement seems too insignificant to send a person to hell for; well, the sad news is that many are in judgment already because of it.

From the time of Cain and Abel, murder has always being considered a most evil act by society. Even with the dispensation of grace, those who commit murder are viewed as more evil than others. Our societies reject them, and they are usually not given any chance to step back into the community to express their remorse.

But Jesus came and spoke to a group of people and made it clear that there is no difference between a person who has committed murder and a person who says to his brother, "You are a fool." Before God, not only he who has committed murder will be judged, but also he who insults his brother will be judged. He came to settle the misconception carried by society that only those who have committed murder will be judged. He was very clear in this: if you are angry at your brother, you are equally as guilty as a murderer, and both will be judged.

One may analyze and ask questions: Is this, really, not a bit harsh on us? Mean, you did not kill anyone, you were only angry at the one who has offended you. How then are you given the same verdict as a murderer?

Look at it this way. If somebody has wronged you and you managed to hold yourself from murdering that person, this means you have succeeded already. Now, what makes it hard for you to let it go? The thing here is not the offence you committed; rather, it is the length of time that the offensive action resided in your heart, soul, and spirit. This is what leads you to judgment—not the offence, but the way you handled the offence.

Jesus ensured that we would inherit His kingdom when He allowed Himself to be nailed to the cross. He absorbed all accounts of evil without holding anything against anyone.

This is what makes God view murder, anger, grudges, and insults as acts that come from the same source—the devil. He did not have these features of evil when He went to the cross. He did not have them even after the cross, and He does not have them even today. So the question is, why does man possess these features? Where do they come from? The period of time you allow anger and insults to reside in your heart reveals the extent of evil nature you possess.

Ephesians 4:1–3: *"I therefore, a prisoner for the Lord, urge you to walk in a manner worthy of the calling to which you have been called, with all humility and gentleness, with patience, bearing with one another in love, eager to maintain the unity of the Spirit in the bond of peace."*

If you walk by all these attributes of the Spirit, there is no way anger can reside in your heart for a long period of time. If the spirit of God lives in you, it will not share its place with evil. The love that abounds in you will maintain the unity of the spirit in the bond of peace.

The extent of anger a person carries varies from person to person, but those who are spiritually inclined to the cross always carry their problems to the Lord, and in the process experience a rebirth and the ability to forgive, and this happens every time they encounter offences. That is why it is important to have a constant relationship with the Spirit of God.

Consequently, those who walk by the flesh can remain angry with a person for years and end up being consumed by evil. God distinguishes evil from good, and does not consider the nature of offence committed.

Do not allow the devil to deceive you by telling you that the measure of sin or offence you have committed is not as bad as someone else's offence. Anger is punishable just as much as murder, and they both have the same consequence: hellfire. Today, purpose in your heart to let it all go. It might not seem worth it, but it is. Is that person you hold in your heart worth what Christ has done for you? Absolutely not. Your destiny cannot be terminated by a person when Christ has guaranteed it.

Deuteronomy 31:12: *"Be careful to do all the words of this law."*

As a believer, it is very important to be careful to keep the word of the Lord—the law. To be careful is to be alert and watchful that you do not break any laws of the Lord.

First John 3:5: *"In Him [Christ] there is no sin."*

Because there is no sin in Christ, you should live your life the same way. Allow the blood of Jesus Christ to take away those sins you regarded as small, and begin a new relationship with Christ. A sin-free believer is a God-fearing believer, and a God-fearing believer makes great achievements. Greatness is triggered by the ability to set aside what causes smallness. Being unable to forgive causes you to be in a low position, and it is in that state that you are bound to sin. May the grace of our Lord Jesus Christ abound in you in order that you may hold nothing but the love of God in your heart.

"Do It, But Not Too Much"

Deuteronomy 6:5: *"You shall love the Lord your God with all your heart and with all your soul and with all your might."*

Are you loving the Lord, but not with all your heart? Are you working for the Lord, but not with all your might? Then make up your mind to dedicate your entire life to Him, because what He holds for you is mind blowing. You will never give a mind-blowing testimony until you give a mind-blowing service.

Revelations 3:16: *"So, because you are lukewarm, and neither hot nor cold, I will spit you out of my mouth."*

There are no two ways about love; it is either you work hard to sustain it, or whatever lame effort you offer will collapse it in a matter of time. Love does not work by itself; rather, it is kept with deeds.

We are living in times in which the secular world has taken over the place of the Lord in our lives. If you look at where that comes from closely, you will realize that one of the factors that contribute to man abandoning his services to God arises from a small whisper: "It is too much. You can't continue to do that for God." This voice makes a lot of people take a backseat in God's kingdom, as they convince themselves that they have done too much for God and they should now reduce their work for God's kingdom.

The reality of the matter is that you cannot feel or see all the effects of God's messages in operation now or here on earth, but sometimes in our lives, or even after we have departed, part of the scriptures will be revealed, and we will experience that God's message of love was and is not a choice but an obligation you should or could have honored. How you live your life now will determine how God will relate to you tomorrow and in the life to come.

Matthew 25:41: *"Then he will say to those on his left, 'Depart from me, you cursed, into the eternal fire prepared for the devil and his angels.'"*

The Lord Jesus has authority over all things, and in our current life we should live only to impress Him. Many do not impress God, but live to impress their employers or the government, compromising the government of Christ. Eternal life is inherited by faith in Christ Jesus, and not in anyone else.

Some people are doing their level best to impress their employers at the expense of others. Others work very hard to be promoted and to have a good name before kings and queens. Even in churches some believers work to impress their pastors, working tirelessly for man but forsaking the Lord. The rewards we get in this lifetime are perishable, and they are all earthly. And even earthly rewards come from no man. We all need to work hard in order to support our families and to live a better life.

Psalm 75:5–6: *"'Do not lift up your horn on high, or speak with haughty neck.' For not from the east or from the west and not from the wilderness comes lifting up."*

Most people are blowing their own horns in an attempt to be promoted. They think it is the sound they make that will attract favor. It is not even how kind and soft-spoken you are to your supervisor that will bring elevation. And some assume is how often they bring good tidings before the priest that will grant them promotion. Not even good works brings uplift. To guarantee your promotion, focus your attention on God—the one who issues promotions. It is a waste of time to focus on man. The Bible says there is no stiff-necked person who brings promotion. If the Lord is ready to lift you up, no one can prevent it no matter how stiff necked they are, and this is what the Lord is doing in your life. He has placed you among stiff-necked people for a reason, so that He shows that no one has the capacity to promote except Him. And you will witness His word coming to pass. All those stiff-necked demons will wonder how you got to the top. And the Lord will break open all those difficult doors that do not want to open for you. Sometimes in life you need to be employed in the company of hardhearted people who will do everything to prevent you from reaching the top. Give them space to do their things. Allow them to render your name useless to those who occupy higher positions. They are not aware that they are contributing to your promotion. They are not aware that, through their evil deeds, the Lord will deem you fit for promotion. Even if you did not qualify for promotion, because of their evil, they will qualify you before the Lord. No man can suppress what the Lord has supplied. The Lord is supplying you with the grace to work for Him with all of your strength, and that strength will open doors for you.

This is the time for you to make up your mind and serve the Lord with all of your strength and with all of your heart. It is because of such dedication that many have been deceived by the devil that serving the Lord with all your might is not worth it. That can never be true! Serving the Lord with all of your soul and all of your might will never be too much if you understand who God is. If you understand that you exist in Him, and He possesses all your requirements needed for you to qualify for you to be uplifted and promoted, serving Him will not be a problem. In fact, you and the Lord will be one, and all that He has will be yours.

First Timothy 4:10: *"For to this end we toil and strive, because we have our hope set on the living God, who is the Savior of all people, especially of those who believe."*

The Apostle Paul was writing to Timothy about the type of conduct that he should display as a servant of Christ Jesus. He said; *"for this end we toil and strive"* not for earthly things, but for godliness. It is not easy to attain godliness, and it is even more difficult to attain it fully; that is, with all of your might. There are people in life who wake up each and every single day to attain godliness and still they can't find themselves at a point at which they are satisfied, just like the Apostle Paul. And there are those who sometimes remember that they should toil and strive to attain godliness. If the Apostle Paul, a man who walked with the power of the Holy Spirit, strove and toiled daily for godliness, we should expect to strive and toil even more, especially in these times of great evil. Are you not supposed to work much harder for the Lord, with all of your heart, soul, and might? Are you not supposed to rely on Him to lead you in the right direction? In these end times, strive and toil for godliness and forsake the world. Only then will the Lord lift you to greater heights. Only then will there be no need for you to depend on man for your promotion.

First Corinthians 9:24: *"Do you not know that in a race all runners compete, but only one receives the prize? So run that you may obtain it."*

How are you running your race in your relationship with the Lord? Are you running in a manner that will enable you to receive the prize? If not, then it is by grace that you are reminded that you are a potential winner. Nobody is competing against you, and you are not competing against anybody, but we are individually competing against the things that prevent us from seeing the glory of Lord. God has equipped you to outrun them. You are equipped to outrun doubt, fear, unbelief, sickness, debt, lust, violence, hate, and love of money. These are the things that you are competing against. The Lord is telling you to receive that prize today that prize …the prize of boldness, faith, love, greatness, peace, wealth, and grace, for you are born a victor. This is your true identity … the identity that the Lord has given to you. Receive it into your spirit, and your life will never be the same.

"I Will Repent Later"

Matthew 21:28–29: *"What do you think? A man had two sons. And he went to the first and said, 'Son, go and work in the vineyard today.' And he answered, 'I will not,' but afterward he changed his mind and went. And he went to the other son and said the same. And he answered, 'I go, sir,' but did not go."*

Jesus told a parable about two sons. One initially refused to go to work in his father's vineyard, but later changed his mind. The other initially agreed to work in the vineyard but did not go. The question is, which one did the will of his father? And they answered, "The one who later changed his mind." But there are those who claim that they have repented; meanwhile, their works tells a different story. Jesus Christ said that it is better to say you can't and then later change your mind and do rather than to say you can do something and then not do it. Believers assume there is no harm when they agree to assist in outreach and evangelism and later sit at home without following up with those to whom they were assigned. Sometimes you think, well, it is not such a big deal to make promises and not fulfill them.

Matthew 21:31–32: *"Truly, I say to you, the tax collectors and the prostitutes go into the kingdom of God before you. For John came to you in the way of righteousness, and you did not believe him, but the tax collectors and the prostitutes believed him. And even when you saw it, you did not afterward change your minds and believe him."*

The point that Jesus is making is that "righteous" people could not right away believe the message that John brought, but tax collectors and prostitutes, even though they were not on the right path, changed, and they believed John. This is the case in the churches today; it is as if the message of salvation, repentance, and faith is preached to prostitutes, thieves, and tax collectors but not believers. "Righteous" people take a very long time to accept and believe the power of Christ, because they are too familiar with the whole salvation affair and "how God operates." This is how we miss the actions of God. We take a long time to say, "Yes, Lord, I believe that you can make someone great out of me. Come into my life and refresh my soul." This is the devil at work. Nobody can say, "I know God", for no one has seen Him. We see Him at work and still we can't be familiar with His acts, for no one knows His thoughts. Take each and every message of God with sincerity as if you are hearing it for the last time. Make it a habit to hear Him when you are rebuked, and never again live a life of disobedience.

Colossians 3:1–2: *"If then you have been raised with Christ, seek the things that are above, where Christ is, seated at the right hand of God. Set your minds on things that are above, not on things that are on earth."*

People who take time to repent or who take time to work on their salvation are people who have set their minds on the things of the world. Why do you set your minds on that which will not benefit you? All things that you see are perishable, but the things of God that you do not see are the ones that will stand. That is why the word of God says, to set our minds on such things. But because some people think they are not spirit beings, they believe they can't make an impact in the spiritual world. There are two things that can happen to man: he can either discover that he is a spirit being when he is on earth, or he can discover that he is a spirit being when he leaves this world. One way or the other, you will discover the spiritual impact you possess. Those who have lived on this earth and have passed on are discovering the spiritual power they possessed which they did not put to use. Spiritual powers are for everyone, but the difference comes when you have to choose which kingdom you want to operate from. Choose and put then God's kingdom first. Then whatever impact you want to make will be granted to you. Make up your mind to think about the things that are above, which are of God, and by so doing you will experience a divine intervention in a special and unique way.

Second Timothy 3:1–6: *"But understand this, that in the last days … People will … be having the appearance of godliness, but denying its power."*

This means that in the last days, some people will speak well of the Lord Jesus Christ, accepting Him and proclaiming that they know Him, but yet rejecting and denying the power of His spirit. Such people are the ones who say that there is a God, but they do nothing for that God. They are the ones who say they know the Holy Spirit but refuse fellowship with the same Spirit. With their mouths they say "Yes, Lord" but with their actions they say "No, Lord!" The appearances of such people is convincing to an extent that they are placed in high positions in churches and later lead the flock astray; it is their fruits that tell of their intentions.

Proverbs 11:30: *"The fruit of the righteous is a tree of life, and whoever captures souls is wise."*

A fruit can become a tree if its seeds are captured and planted in fertile ground. If someone claims he is hearing from God, check to see if he has the fruit of righteousness. Is he winning souls for Christ? Does winning souls mean that we should force people to God's kingdom? No, but it means to minister God's words. Do you know of people who have been born again for many years but have never shared a single scripture with you? If you do, pray for them that they should not only attain a form of godliness, but that they should put what they believe in into action.

Revelations 2:5: *"Remember therefore from where you have fallen; repent, and do the works you did at first. If not, I will come to you and remove your lamp stand from its place, unless you repent."*

What the Lord means is that, if you don't repent, you won't be able to see where you are and where you are going. No one can see when the lamp stand has been taken from its place. The place that the Lord is talking about is the place where you have fallen; this is where you should repent, at a place where you have sinned. This means that you should repent immediately after you have transgressed. If you make fewer steps to attempt to walk without repenting, the lamp stand will be taken away from you, and you will walk alone with the absence of the Spirit of the Lord. After you have repented, keep up with your repentance so that you may bear fruit. Is there a reward for repentance? Yes,

Mathew 3:8: *"Bear fruits in keeping with repentance."*

Repentance produces the fruit of the spirit.

Galatians 5:22–23: *"Love, joy, peace, patience, kindness, goodness, faithfulness, gentleness, self control ..."*

Therefore be cautious with your repentance so that you will be able to walk with the Lord. Pray to God that He will grant you His grace to walk in righteousness, as it is the Lord's will for you.

"His Grace is Sufficient"

Second Corinthians 12:8–9: *"Three times I pleaded with the Lord about this, that it should leave me. But he said to me, 'My grace is sufficient for you, for my power is made perfect in weakness.'"*

Grace is conditional, but some believers don't want to agree to this; hence, they live their Christianity under deception. We were all saved by grace (Ephesians 2:5), but that should not render the grace unconditional. For the mere fact that you were saved and there are other people who are not saved tells you that grace is conditional, and the conditions of your salvation are known to God. Other believers don't often talk about the conditions that are attached to the grace of the Lord, and this is what the devil wants—an ignorant believer. Today the grace of God is spoken of as something outside of Christ. Is it Christ first, then grace? Or grace first, then Christ? We sometimes forget that the grace of God is found in Christ.

Have you considered why God told the Apostle Paul that His grace was sufficient? The reason was that Paul's walk was pleasing before Him. Not once but three times did Paul plead with God. This tells you that Paul had a strong relationship with the Lord. It is then the Lord revealed to Paul that His grace was sufficient. That revelation did not just come by itself; rather, it was earned. He did not plead once or twice, but three times, and these are conditions that are attached to the grace. Paul teaches us that you should always plead with the Lord for His grace to be sufficient in your life. Yes, grace is the unmerited favor of the Lord, but if you want to maintain that grace, you should please the one who favors you without merit. Grace is not an obvious effort extended by the Lord over each believer; you must plead with the Lord over your matters in order for you to receive grace. Even for other people to be saved, it was somebody or some congregation that somewhere had to plead with the Lord for souls. If they had decided to refrain from interceding, many could have been led astray. Plead with the Lord for His grace of salvation over your family, over lost souls, for a faithful Christian walk, and for your spiritual growth. Plead with the Lord, and His response will be, "My child, there is enough grace for you to excel." His grace is indeed sufficient for you to keep on believing in that breakthrough, and that in the flesh will be the thing of the past.

Do not sit there and confess the grace without pleasing the Lord by living right while the devil is tampering with your life. Change your mentality and begin to plead with the Lord concerning your case. It is a deception when you think that the sufficient grace of the Lord is without efforts from you towards God. Yes, the grace of the Lord falls on every individual God chooses, but sustaining it is a different thing.

Second Corinthians 12:10: *"For the sake of Christ, then, I am content with weakness …"*

Paul was content with weakness not because weakness had overwhelmed him, but for the sake of Christ and hence God's grace became sufficient over his life, Hallelujah! What grace, then, are you waiting for if you have accepted Christ but you don't live to sustain that grace? Revive your heart today, and live your life for the sake of Christ and, insults, hardships, persecution, or calamities will never shatter God's purpose over your life. Play your part in sustaining God's grace over your life, and you will also speak like Paul in 2 Corinthians 12:10: *"For when I am weak, then I am strong."*

Become a unique Christian who prays and asks for grace over the nation. Put your entire mind in Christ and make all your ways pleasing before Him, and He will have no other option but to show up in your weakness.

Second Corinthians 12:9: *"For my power is made perfect in weakness."*

Are you weak and expect an encounter with God? Then you are a fertile ground in which God can demonstrate His power over your life. The grace of God is falling on you now, receive it! God is visiting your state of affairs. His grace of healing is coming over you and those you know. His grace of miracles, signs, and wonders is falling on you. If all is well with you, God will never be seen clearly, but when things are blurry, your testimony is at hand. The Grace of God exists in Christ, because Christ is the demonstration of God's grace. He answers your requests, and He grants your petitions. Prepare yourself to be uplifted, for there is no power under the sun or in the heavens that can put down the one upon whom the grace of the Lord has fallen. People have been sick to a point of death, experiencing different forms of bodily destruction, with everybody giving up hope for them, but when the grace of God found them, they became the mouth of the Lord, testifying of the greatness of the Lord.

If you are experiencing this state of weakness, whether emotional, physical, or spiritual, there is one thought that you should never entertain, and that is that it is all over. The devil knows that the grace of God is there for you. That is why he convinces believers that grace will fall on their laps. Many other weaker people have never had the opportunity to experience the fullness of God's grace in their lives simply because they were made to believe that grace is out there waiting for them. What, then, is that perfect power of God? It is Christ Himself. Christ is that perfect power of God (Colossians 1:15–16). He is the image of the invincible God, the firstborn of all creation, for by Him all things were created. When you have Christ in you, you have God's perfect power. He is the firstborn of all creation, things that are seen and all that is not seen.

The grace of God is found in Christ, and by Him all things were created. This means that, if you are in need of something and it's not there, Christ will create it for you. If someone manipulated your promotion at work, there is no need for you to worry yourself when you are in Christ, because Christ will create your new position. Christ excels in creation. When you feel that any part of your body needs to be replaced, He is the Creator; by Him all things were created. Therefore, serve your Creator well, and you will lack nothing.

"Others managed; I'll also manage"

Acts 19:11–16: *"And God was doing extraordinary miracles by the hands of Paul, so that even handkerchiefs or aprons that had touched his skin were carried away to the sick, and their diseases left them and the evil spirits came out of them. Then some of the itinerant Jewish exorcists undertook to invoke the name of the Lord Jesus over those who had evil spirits, saying, 'I adjure you by the Jesus whom Paul proclaims.' Seven sons of a Jewish high priest named Sceva were doing this. But the evil spirit answered them, 'Jesus I know, and Paul I recognize, but who are you?' And the man in whom was the evil spirit leaped on them, mastered all of them and overpowered them, so that they fled out of that house naked and wounded."*

Have you ever commanded your finances to be under your control, and after you have prayed and made declarations in the name of Jesus, the situation became worse than before? Or have you ever prayed for your marriage to be stable and full of love, and after you have made that prayer something evil barged into the house like a whirlwind? You will ask yourself, "Where have I failed? Is the name of the Lord Jesus functioning?" And you will conclude by deciding you do not qualify. No way! That is a lie from the pit of hell. The name of the Lord is for everyone who calls unto Him for help. The name of Jesus Christ is a very powerful name that destroys every work of evil. But there is something that you should learn to do in order to make that name work; in other words, you should be licensed to use the name of Jesus.

James 4:2: *"You desire and do not have, so you murder. You covet and cannot obtain, so you fight and quarrel. You do not have, because you do not ask. You ask and do not receive because, you ask wrongly, to spend it on your passions."*

The seven sons of Sceva had no relationship with the Lord Jesus Christ. They were sons of a religious priest who did not know how to use the name of Jesus to prevent the operation of the kingdom of darkness over their circumstances. Thus, to his sons, the name *Jesus* was just a religion; hence, the demons retaliated and overpowered them because they were so empty in the word and in the revelation of the power behind the name of Jesus. The sons of Sceva used the name of Jesus to see if it would work for them or not. They used the name Jesus for themselves and not to glorify the Lord, and this is what some believers do. If you desire to possess something because you envy someone, and you pray for a visitation of the Lord, you have an answer already; and that is, you will not receive. And, just like the sons of Sceva, if you ask with such a mentality, a serious attack from the kingdom of darkness will be raised against you. But when you pray sincerely, the attack you encounter after praying is just a manifestation of evil, revealing to you what was hidden. Pray persistently, and you shall receive your answer. Your motive for prayer is what makes the difference.

First John 2:16: *"For all that is in the world—the desires of the flesh and the desires of the eyes and the pride in possessions—is not from the Father but is from the world."*

The devil makes you believe that you can achieve what others have achieved and you can manage good things as well as others do. He makes people attempt to cast out demons, because they saw someone casting out demons. He makes it a point that you measure your life with what others possess. Jesus commissioned every believer to cast out demons. That's right—Jesus. If, then, you don't commit yourself to His word, you will pay the price in return.

It is not wrong to sometimes aspire to be like other successful believers or to see yourself as the next great man of God. But, if your motives are not correct, your requests will be in vain.

Matthew 16:13–19: *"Now when Jesus came into the district of Caesarea Philippi, he asked his disciples, 'Who do people say that the Son of Man is?' And they said, 'Some say John the Baptist, others say Elijah, and others Jeremiah or one of the prophets.' He said to them, 'But who do you say that I am?' Simon Peter replied, 'You are the Christ, the Son of the living God.' And Jesus answered him, 'Blessed are you, Simon Bar-Jonah! For flesh and blood has not revealed this to you, but my Father who is in heaven. And I tell you, you are Peter, and on this rock I will build my church, and the gates of hell shall not prevail against it. I will give you the keys of the kingdom of heaven.'"*

After the living God revealed who Christ was to Simon, Jesus said *"And I tell you, you are Peter ..."* Do you think that Jesus did not know who Peter was? He knew; He was just reassuring Peter and making him realize what his true identity was. Jesus was reassuring Peter, because he got his revelation from the living God and not from what others said. This is what

Jesus requires from each and every one of us. The first thing that you must do so that Jesus can make you realize who you are is to seek a revelation of who He is. You need that revelation, because it is from there that you will experience a turnaround and a realization of self. When you receive a revelation of who Jesus is, and your life is based on that revelation, you will receive a word that reveals your true identity and an expanded mandate in God's kingdom.

Jesus said to Peter, when Jesus had been revealed to him, *"I will build my church, and the gates of hell shall not prevail against it."* The revelation that was from God to Peter linking him to Jesus so that his destiny could be released.

Today! Jesus is revealing your true identity to your spirit, and it is through that identity that your assignment will be established. Seek a revelation of who Jesus is from the Lord. Do not depend on what others are saying or have gained or have possessed. God is releasing a unique mandate for you, a special type of gift that will cause the world to marvel …a higher anointing designed for you for this end time. Refrain from looking at what others are managing, and allow God to give you your unique possessions.

If the word of God says you are an ambassador of His kingdom, you must live like one. If He says you are an heir of the royal priesthood, conduct yourself like one, for if that revelation is written about you in His word, the gates of hell shall not prevail against it. The devil will not conquer what God says about you from His word. No demon will prevail against the church. Who is the church? You! You are the church of God Christ is talking about. In other words, the gates of hell will not prevail against the works of your hands, the steps you take, and the intentions you want to pursue. Where you are there will be prosperity, abundance, success, and stability simply because the gates of hell cannot prevail against you.

When God says you are the head and not the tail, you are, whether you are the least to be recognized or not. Possess your future by what God reveals to you, not by what people are saying. Do not measure your life with the measure of man, for no man is higher than God. Measure your life based on what the heavens have decided about you. When the boardroom says a word that is different from what the heavens are saying, which word will you believe—the one from the gathering in the boardroom or the one from the gathering in the heavens? Which gathering is positioned higher than the other? And how high is it situated?

Peter never became confused by what others were saying about Christ—what people said about Jesus as if they knew Him. Many would believe their testimony about Jesus. Their confessions of who Jesus was were so close that no one would see anything wrong about Jesus being one of the great prophets of old, but He was not what they said He was. He was greater than everything people said of Him. Look, don't go to and fro. When you seek God's fresh heavenly revelations, He will grant them to you, and this shall rescue many from ignorance. Your testimony will be a life-changing one, and your achievement will never go unnoticed. Those who thought they were ahead of you will be behind you, for God's revelation will form a fresh foundation for your life. Do not compare yourself with any man, but measure your life from what He has revealed about you from His word.

"Tempted by God"

Romans 6:16: *"Do you know that if you present yourselves to anyone as obedient slaves, you are slaves of the one whom you obey ..."*

The moment you give in and present yourself to evil you have become an obedient slave to it. If you come across evil, it is not God who allowed you to fall into sin, but it is the extent of your resistance to sin that has failed you. Anytime you come across evil, if the measure of knowledge of God's word you have in your spirit is less than the measure of evil you encounter, you are likely to commit sin.

James 1:13–14: *"Let no one say when he is tempted, 'I am being tempted by God,' for God cannot be tempted with evil, and he himself tempts no one. But each person is tempted where he is lured and enticed by his own desire."*

Matthew 6:13: *"And lead us not into temptation …"*

This is what Jesus taught His disciples. Does this mean that God can lead a person to temptation? Absolutely not! Ask yourself this question: is there a person who will overcome the temptations that the Lord leads him into, if God truly is the one who leads man into temptation? Nobody can survive those temptations. But because He knows each one's weakness, He equipped man with relevant attributes to overcome every manner of evil he encounters, with the relevant measure he can withhold or withstand. This means that evil will always come your way, but it is your responsibility to make sure that you don't fall into sin.

Jesus looked at God as the one who sustains a believer through temptations and also as the one who grants the grace to overcome it. That is, God gives you the capacity for you to survive through temptation. Now, the words *"lead us not into temptation"* speak more about God giving you, as the supremacy, the ability to overcome temptations. The devil has made many people believe that God leads His people into temptation, making them easily allow themselves to be tempted and fall into sin without resisting it. How can you involve God when you willingly and deliberately enter into sin?

Matthew 6:8: *"Do not be like them, for your Father knows what you need before you ask him."*

God knows everything about you, even before you ask. He knows everything. There is no way He can lead you into temptation. The only problem that some have is that they don't pray to God to help them through their temptations.

Matthew 6:41: *"Watch and pray that you may not enter into temptation. The spirit indeed is willing, but the flesh is weak."*

The temptations you come across can be overcome by only one thing: prayer. God has the ability to give you the grace to carry your body and begin to pray.

Roman 7:15: *"I do not understand my actions. For I do not do what I want ..."*

Temptation can take effect in your life when you don't understand your actions, and when you do things anyhow and waste your strength on unprofitable activities. It's your actions that justify your commitment to resist temptation. The things you want to do you don't do, and the things you don't want to do you do. God is therefore not responsible for evil actions, but He becomes delighted when your actions glorify His holy name.

Proverbs 16:25: *"There is a way which seems right to a man ..."*

This way appears straight to a man who is led into temptation. If a way appears straight, however it is actually crooked, and that's a deception. You are being deceived by the devil to walk that way.

First Samuel 15:1–3: *"And Samuel said to Saul, 'The Lord sent me to anoint you king over his people Israel; now therefore listen to the words of the Lord. Thus says the Lord of hosts, "I have noted what Amalek did to Israel in opposing them on the way when they came up out of Egypt. Now go and strike Amalek and devote to destruction all that they have. Do not spare them, but kill both man and woman, child and infant, ox and sheep, camel and donkey."'"*

First Samuel 15:9–11: *"But Saul and the people spared Agag and the best of the sheep and of the oxen and of the fattened calves and the lambs, and all that was good, and would not utterly destroy them. All that was despised and worthless they devoted to destruction. The word of the Lord came to Samuel: 'I regret that I have made Saul king, for he has turned back from following me and has not performed my commandments.'"*

Saul was tempted by the fattened calves and lambs that the Amalekites had. God had already commanded what he should do when he attacked the Amalekites. God commanded him to destroy everything, and Saul's response was that he would destroy only the worthless ones. Is this not what other ministers do? Embrace those who are wealthy and yet forsaken by the Lord?

Saul decided to destroy everything that was worthless and despised and keep for himself all that was good. This was not what God had commanded him to do. Saul also spared the Amalekite king, Agag. Agag held the highest position of power in the kingdom of the Amalekites, and he was spared by Saul. This king should have been the first one to be destroyed, because he was the leader and the main reason God wanted to destroy the Amalakites. This king possessed all the strategies of evil that God wanted to abolish, but Saul, the opposing king, kept him. Saul spared Agag; he did not destroy the evil that could have been uprooted. Agag was taken into the camp of the Israelites, his deceptive and evil traits would follow him and spread among the children of God and later influence them and lead them into destruction. And this made the Lord regret ever making Saul a king, because of his ignorance.

In your walk with God, make sure that you don't allow your fleshly desires to tempt you to spare what God said you should destroy. Avoid carrying into your destiny habits that the Lord commanded you get rid of. If you know that you rely on corruption or you have other bad habits that you have spared, understand that you can't take that into phase of greatness. If you do, the Lord will remove you from your rulership as king or manager. Some believers are easily tempted by money, clothes, cars, and many other things that lead to temptation, because of the fleshly desires they possess. The desire to have good things makes it easy to forget what God has commanded in His word. And the desire to live a flourishing life of wealth and pleasure tempts many people and later leads them into sin.

This, then, makes us come to a point of self-realization of what God wants. God cannot give out commands of how we should conduct our lives and later tempt us into doing evil; is not like that. We are all led into temptation by our fleshy desires to possess and to have access to the things that do not belong to us. Surrender all to the Lord. Destroy all your bad habits. Do not spare any, and allow God to take over from there.

Second Thessalonians 2:13–14: *"God chose you as the first fruits to be saved, through sanctification by the Spirit and belief in the truth. To this he called you through our gospel, so that you may obtain the glory of our Lord Jesus Christ."*

Christ Himself was tempted, not by fleshy desires, but by God's glory to give hope to man. Through Christ, man is set free from all desires of the flesh. The temptations of Christ were that of the devil, who wanted Christ to abandon His mandate, so the devil could take it from there.

Matthew 4:1: *"Then Jesus was led up by the spirit into the wilderness to be tempted by the devil."*

Christ was so filled with the spirit of God that, when He was tempted by evil, He overcame that temptation. He was filled with God's glory.

Temptation to Him was a platform on which He could demonstrate God's glory. Jesus wanted to show the devil that He had already made up His mind to save all those who were lost, and He was not prepared to lose that chance over a simple demonstration that would prove His power to the devil. Even to us, temptation must be an opportunity for God to give us a pat on the back and say, "Well done, my child. You have done well."

This will only be possible when you have allowed the spirit of God to take over your life and to guide you in all that you do. When temptation comes, thank God for that opportunity to prove your love to Him for the name of the Lord will be glorified. Hallelujah!

"God Understands"

Titus 2:7–8: *"Show yourself in all respects to be a model of good works, and in your teaching show integrity, dignity, and sound speech that cannot be condemned, so that an opponent may be put to shame, having nothing evil to say about us."*

There is not a single point in life at which God will understand if we decide to live our lives outside of holiness. We find today our lives in a terrible state of agony simple because the principles of God have been compromised under the deception that "God understands." Some believers do not pay their tithe because they claim that God understands; others do not fast because they claim that God understands; some go to the extent of refusing to fellowship with other Christians, because they claim that God understands that they should be on their own, having fellowship with the Holy Spirit at home.

Paul, being aware of such conduct among Christians, wrote to Titus to give him guidance with regard to how he should conduct himself as a servant of Christ. He mentioned that Titus was a model of good works. Why? Because people were observing his conduct. His emphasis was on putting the opponents to shame, and focusing on not doing anything that could give people the opportunity to say anything evil about him. Now imagine how many people would disqualify you as a Christian if they knew you had committed evil even though you say you are a believer? People's words don't matter, but our conduct toward them matters. In order to win people to Christ, our approach toward life should always display good conduct before God and man.

God does not understand a believer who deliberately forsakes his responsibilities and begins to follow some doctrine that is not in line with His word. Some people substitute God's grace with tradition, because they are deceived into believing that God understands. Your life is a mirror image of your soul to the world. The things that you go through must elevate you to greatness and not tear you apart.

Luke 1:46–48: *"And Mary said, 'My soul magnifies the Lord, and my spirit rejoices in God my Savior, for he has looked on the humble estate of his servant.'"*

Humility is a key to your uplift to the kingdom. Your soul should magnify the Lord. Christ should be the only one who is lifted in all things. Christians who have excuses about their service to God are simply Christians who are not humble before the Lord. When you think of the Lord, your spirit must be filled with joy, for you know that God looks on the humble estate of His servant.

Mary, the mother of Jesus, looked forward with anticipation to her unborn son as her Savior. That's humility at its highest degree—a mother calling her unborn child a savior. Some parents have been hearing the word of

God for a very long time, but when their children come with the light, they refuse to see because they are not humble. That is why God had to use a humble woman to bring Jesus to earth. That tells you a lot about humility. It is a place in which God desires you to dwell. If you often miss church thinking that God understands, are you not transferring your blessing to those who are more dedicated to the Lord? Are you a double-minded believer? Seek the face of the Lord more and prevent the devil from deceiving you.

Luke 16:7–10: *"Will any one of you who has a servant plowing or keeping sheep say to him when he has come in from the field, 'Come at once and recline at table'? Will he not rather say to him, 'Prepare supper for me, and dress properly, and serve me while I eat and drink, and afterward you will eat and drink'? Does he thank the servant because he did what was commanded? So you also, when you have done all that you were commanded, say, 'We are unworthy servants; we have only done what was our duty.'"*

Jesus spoke of a servant who served his master until the master became satisfied. In this parable, He describes a servant as a person who waited on his master without expecting any compliment thereafter, simply because it was the duty of the servant to serve. Ask yourself, what kind of servant are you? Are you consistent with the master's commands? Do you satisfy your master with your services? We live in times of evolution of many doctrines with a great followership … times of patterns that are initiated and practiced, and standards that are set and maintained. Should they compromise our fellowship with Christ? Absolutely not.

If there is one thing that is draining the spirit of Christ, that would be rebellion. The fear of the Lord is not there; we fear people more than we fear Him. You are called to prepare supper for Him, and it is a great honor given to you by the Lord to prepare God's table. We should talk like that women in Matthew 15:27 who said that, even if she didn't eat from the master's table, she could still have a taste of her master's food from the crumbs that fell from the table. Fellow Christians, God does not understand when we do not give our best to Him.

Malachi 3:10: *"Bring the full tithe into the storehouse …"*

Ask yourself, why does God expect you to pay your tithes into a storehouse, a place of abundant supply …a place that has plenty to give from? This does not make sense to others. Here is a place of abundance, full of supply. Why give tithes into a storehouse, and not to any other house? What for?

Believers are very strange people; they walk by faith, not by sight. They believe in things that are not there as if they are there. This means that tithing is also an act of faith. When you give out its full measure, you contribute to the storehouse from which God will supply all your needs. A storehouse is God's place filled with all things that are necessary for you to survive. This makes your tithe a relevant instigator to your divine purpose.

Besides tithing, God also encourages fellowship.

Acts 2:42–44: *"And they devoted themselves to the apostles' teachings and fellowship, to the breaking of bread and the prayers. And awe came upon every soul, and many wonders and signs were being done through the apostles. And all who believed were together and had all things in common."*

The church is established by the Lord, and it is through fellowship among believers that the teaching and preaching of God's word is practiced. The reason for this is that all who believe should stay together and do all things in common. Have you ever asked yourself why churches are splitting into halves? This is because the church of God is not together, and things are not done in common. This, however, does not exempt believers from attending. It does not allow them to stay at home and refuse to fellowship with other believers. God does not understand segregation and will never understand it, because He established fellowship among believers, and it must stand as long as the church is awaiting the second coming of Jesus Christ.

Some people hide themselves over conflicts in churches, and they use this as an excuse to refrain from attending services. If you have reached that state, then the devil has deceived you. No one has ever established a church except God. No one has ever died for your sins except Jesus Christ.

And no spirit has the power to lead the churches except the Holy Spirit. This means that the moment you refrain from the fellowship of believers, you are refusing the ministration of the Holy Spirit over your life. Other believers have in mind that God in His holy nature made food for the body to be edible at all times. This belief makes them believe there is no need for fasting.

Mark 9:28–29: *"And when he had entered the house, his disciples asked him privately, 'Why could we not cast it out?' And he said to them, 'This kind cannot be driven out by anything but prayer.'"*

Matthew 17:21: *"But this kind does not come out except by prayer and fasting"* (International Standard Version).

The same demon that keeps people away from fasting is the same kind that does not want to be cast out. This is the same kind of demon that deceives people by making them believe that there is no need to fast, and that God understands when you do not fast. God will never understand it when you are not growing spiritually and your life is stagnant. But all that you have to do is fast and pray to trigger your destiny.

Matthew 9:14–15: *"Then the disciples of John came to him, saying, 'Why do we and the Pharisees fast, but your disciples do not fast?' And Jesus said to them, 'Can the wedding guests mourn as long as the bridegroom is with them?'"*

Why do you think people become excited when they are invited to weddings? Because they are going to be entertained, most especially by the ones who invited them—the bride and the bridegroom. A wedding's entertainment includes a promise that you will be catered for. You will be served and seated at decorated tables. Everything that takes place at a wedding is aimed at making you a happy person. This is what Jesus meant. His disciples had everything because they were surrounded with good things, and there was no need for them to seek them anywhere else.

Jesus's disciples were well catered for spiritually and even physically. Food was there whenever they asked for it. Revelations were there, and miracles were visible everywhere they went. Fresh words from heaven included prophecies, teachings, and preaching. His disciples were lacking absolutely nothing. All these things are provided for those who seek Christ into their lives through fasting and prayer. All these things are gained by prayer and fasting.

Open doors, miracles, signs, and wonders are waiting for those who have made up their minds to enter into a fast. The glory of God is revealed to people who will deny themselves food and set aside worldly living to fast and pray. Jesus was a holy man, and when He was with His disciples, the rays of His glory reflected in their lives simply because they were close to Him and they moved with Him. Also, to those who fast and pray, the glory of God can forever be noticed in their lives. Therefore, fasting attracts God's glory over into our lives; it invites spiritual progress and suppresses manipulation by demons. It delivers us from evil captivity and releases us from bondages just as it did for the disciples of Jesus. They were free from spiritual captivity. It directs God's will and abolishes the devil's deceptions. It paves a way for us and frustrates the power of evil. It protects and gives life to the poor in spirit.

"You Can't Please Everyone"

First Corinthians 10:31–33: *"So, whether you eat or drink, or whatever you do, do all to the glory of God. Give no offense to Jews or to Greeks or to the church of God, just as I try to please everyone in everything I do, not seeking my own advantage, but that of many, that they may be saved."*

Trying to please others is not against God's will. Believers will tell you that they can't visit other houses because the people who live there don't believe in God, or they won't share a meal served at a house of an unbeliever, for it is against the will of God. If, then, all Christians would think like that, don't you think that fewer people would have been saved? The problem sometimes is brought about by people thinking that they might encounter misfortunes through the food they eat in an unbeliever's house.

First Corinthians 10:27: *"If one of the unbelievers invites you to dinner and you are disposed to go, eat whatever is set before you without raising any question."*

Your actions toward sharing your meal with an unbeliever will testify that Christ rules over your life.

Paul was doing this not only for his own advantage, but for the advantage of many, that they might be saved. In other words, he set aside what would benefit himself to make way for what would benefit many. This means that, whenever he visited an unbeliever's house, he tried to do everything he could to please the unbeliever, and to win him over to the Lord by his actions and conduct. Many are saved because of the good impressions left by some believers, and many are lost because of the bad impressions left by some believers. The impression you leave is an important aspect in your Christian walk. Your good deeds presented before others can minister salvation to unbelievers even before you utter a single word from the Bible.

Questioning unbelievers usually leads to arguments that will later develop into quarrels that will pull them away from believing. Does it sound strange to ignore your need and focus on the needs of others? To cater for them even if you don't have enough? To talk well of those who talk poorly of you? To be kind and speak well of those who seek your destruction? These are the impressions believers are expected to leave behind in the minds of those who don't see the light.

Exodus 23:4–5: *"If you meet your enemy's ox or his donkey going astray, you shall bring it back to him. If you see the donkey of one who hates you lying down under its burden, you shall refrain from leaving him with it, you shall rescue it with him."*

How do you respond toward those who tell you that you are a failure and you will never make it, at school or at work? What do you say about them? If you see that a person who does not regard you as anything has a flat tire on his car, would you tell him before he sets off to drive away? If you return to your enemy his donkey that was lost, he will be pleased. Peace will prevail, and the devil will be put to shame. If God expects you to save a donkey, how much more important would it be if you encountered your enemy's child alone, stranded, and desperate. Would you see this as an opportunity to strike? Or would you assist? Now, the devil, knowing that there would be peace and reconciliation between you and your enemy, would say, "You can't please everyone. Stay away and don't mind them. Stop barging into their affairs." If such thoughts come into your mind, know that the deceiver—the devil—is around, and he intends to steal your breakthrough. These are the platforms the Lord has set to elevate you, so learn to tap into such opportunities.

Luke 6:35: *"But love your enemies, and do good, and lend, expecting nothing in return, and your reward will be great, and you will be sons of the Most High."*

When Christ was preaching the Sermon on the Mount, He sat down. This means that He was about to take His time and reveal the secrets that qualify man to be a son or a daughter of the Most High, and inherit blessings from Him. There He made a revelation:

Matthew 5:9: *"Blessed are the peacemakers, for they shall be called sons of God."*

Loving and assisting your enemy is an act of seeking peace; this makes you a peacemaker. And Jesus continued to say that, because you are peacemakers, you will be called the sons of God. If you have a dispute with someone and you do not intend to bring the matter to an end, you shall forfeit your status as a son of God. Sons of God pray for their enemies. They wish them well, and they want to please them as well. Do you want to be a son or a daughter of the Lord? Then, be a peacemaker, and you will be a son of God, and your reward will be great. This means that some people may be rewarded, but your reward, as a peacemaker, will be great. Haven't you asked yourself how great is great before the Lord? This greatness that God talks of is one that is beyond measure. A great reward is one that cannot be explained or defined by man … one that surpasses the understanding of man, and one that cannot be clearly explained and comprehended by man. Sometimes when God talks of a great reward, we think of heaven only. But it's a reward that will start on earth and excite you and connect you to your reward in heaven. All peacemakers are made great by the Lord, and reconciliation attracts and magnifies greatness. God has called you into greatness, and one key is to become a peacemaker. It may appear foolish to those who do not understand God's principles, but to you it is a ladder to great heights. Seek for that opportunity to exercise reconciliation anywhere you go, and your name will be remembered in all places.

"Earthly Conduct Is Not Wrong"

Romans 12:1–2: *"I appeal to you therefore, brothers, by the mercies of God, to present your bodies as a living sacrifice, holy and acceptable to God, which is your spiritual worship. Do not be conformed to this world, but be transformed by the renewal of your mind, that by testing you may discern what is the will of God, what is good and acceptable and perfect."*

A spiritual discernment is a spiritual gift from God, given to all believers for them to use to detect divine truth from error. The gift to discern is not only a gift, but also a spirit.

First Corinthians 2:15: *"The spiritual person judges all things, but is himself to be judged by no one."*

But because of deception, some have sold their ability to conquer evil through discernment. This happens when they allow the world rather than the Spirit to detect good or evil. There is absolutely no way the world can offer to a Christian what is good. It is a son of God who should offer to the world what is good. The world uses eyes to distinguish good from bad, but Christians use the Spirit. The devil, being aware of this truth, blindfolds many so he can use their ears and eyes to separate them from evil. Romans 12:2 clearly states that we should not conform to the standards of the world. These standards include titles, positions, seats, and names. Most unfortunately, there are Christians who are easily influenced by positions and titles. This makes it very difficult for them to have a spirit of discernment. We rely on what we see instead of discerning what is the will of God. This means that people who are easily influenced by appearances find it difficult to do God's will. It won't be possible for you to do God's will if you can't discern the truth, because it is through discernment that you separate what is good from what is evil.

James 2:1: *"My brothers, show no partiality as you hold the faith in our Lord Jesus Christ, the Lord of Glory."*

There is a distinction made in James 2:2– 8between two people. One wears a gold ring and fine clothes, and the other wears shabby clothing. This passage warns us of the danger of concluding what kind of person someone is based upon his appearance. By accepting the one with fine clothing into our midst, over the one with shabby clothing, we have committed a sin.

James 2:9: *"But if you show partiality, you are committing sin."*

Those who show partiality do not have the spirit to discern; hence, they choose to let the one who wears fine linen into their midst. They make this distinction as soon as they have laid their eyes on both men, perceiving the man with shabby clothes to be ungodly and the one with fine linen to be holy and righteous. And on the other hand, when people who discern lay their eyes on both men and receive a word from God regarding whom each one of them is, they are never caught by surprise. The information to them is just a reminder of what they already expected to know. Such people have the grace to win battles before they enter the battle field; their minds are connected to heaven, and they are not easy to bring down. And when they are ultimately down, they are content, for they know it's only a matter of time, and God will visit their course. People who walk in discernment are advanced.

First Peter 1:13–17: *"As obedient children, do not be conformed to the passions of your former ignorance … And if you call on him as Father who judges impartially according to each one's deeds …"*

When we receive the spirit of discernment, we receive God Himself. God is not a God who works with partiality and standards of the world; rather, He is a God who judges our deeds and rewards us accordingly. The spirit to discern is a guarantee of God's presence. And when you experience God's presence in your life, you are no longer conformed to the passions of your former ignorance.

First Peter 1:15: *"But as he who called you is holy, you also be holy."*

Holiness is not being quiet and walking very slowly with your head faced to the ground when you enter church; it is simply not allowing the passions of your former self to govern your life, and setting hope fully on the grace that will reveal Christ's influence over your life. A person who sets his mind fully on Christ is a holy person. Holiness has nothing to do with how you walk.

It is therefore this holiness that will be revealed in your life, because you have not conformed to the standards of the world by showing partiality, by being influenced by titles and positions. You are holy because you know your mind in Christ Jesus.

First John 1:5: *"This is the message we have heard from him and proclaim to you, that God is light, and in him is no darkness at all."*

The message that John brought to the people defined God as light, the One in whom there is no darkness. As God's children, we are filled with that light as well, and we are given the ability to brighten the world. This is the duty and the responsibility of a Christian here on earth. But, then, where is that light in us? You are that light.

Matthew 5:14–15: *"You are the light of the world. A city set on a hill cannot be hidden. Nor do people light a lamp and put it under a basket."*

You are the light; hence, you should not allow the devil to put a basket over your head in order to hide your potential. The devil puts a basket over you by offering you what the world offers. You are not of the world. Your light alone—not collectively with the light of other Christians—is a city set on a hill. You cannot be hidden. No one can hide a city, especially one on top of a hill—a city that everyone can see and that attracts as many people as possible. You cannot be hidden, and you cannot be put away or be dismissed. People can never pretend that they don't see or notice your abilities. You are what people need in order to begin their dreams. Do you still cry and seek help whilst you are the solution? Forget about what the world can offer you, and start focusing on what you can offer the world. You are a city that accommodates many—the rich and the poor, from far and near … a city that provides for people and gives out its product to the needy. The light that comes out of you cannot be compromised for anything. Begin to see yourself like that. Do not allow the world to deceive you with its standards. You are not a little light. You were made to shine and give your light to other neighboring towns. Only a fool with open eyes would say he does not see a city on top of a hill at night. Therefore, don't mind all those who pretend they don't notice your impact. Get going and allow the world see what you have.

"Religon"

Job 13:1–3: *"Behold, my eye has seen all things, my ear has heard and understood it. What you know, I also know; I am not inferior to you. But I would speak to the Almighty, and I desire to argue my case with God."*

What is it that man has come across that would make him ever desire to argue his case with God? Do you feel that you have to speak your mind to Him and get an understanding of all things that you have seen and gone through? In the process of life we want to do our level best to stay away from the things that will hurt us or cause us pain. We ask ourselves, if Jesus is our first and last hope of joy and happiness on earth and in heaven, whom will we turn to if life is treating us poorly? Will we ever gain the trust of this living God? Will we believe that He promised to protect us in all tragedies that are programmed against our lives? You suffer hardships every step of the way, to such an extent that you even begin to doubt this God. It's been a long time since you tasted joy. Now, the difference between a Christian and a non-Christian is that a Christian is sustained by the Holy Spirit in all things he or she comes across. Job felt the need to put everything aside and argue his case before God, because He was the one who saw and heard all things, good and bad. But, the good thing about it all is that Job understood why he had to go through what he went through, and his understanding gave him a word of knowledge.

God is saying to you today that you will understand the reason for everything bad you see with your eyes and everything you hear with your ears—all that distress and pain. And your understanding will give you a word of knowledge. It is through this knowledge that you will assist and encourage the weak and those who will experience the same difficulties you experienced. What is God doing? He is turning your life into an institution of hope for others. He is building you to become a pillar in the area of your pain … a specialist in deliverance and counsel. God is giving you the world so you can offer solutions, and an uplifting spirit in the area of your trial. Today most people who want to encourage others turn to the very life of Job to comfort and to counsel the brokenhearted. Imagine, if Job had not gone through what he went through, we would not have known the wisdom, understanding, and knowledge he gained. The more trials you encounter, the larger your scope of reference. This means that, when you experience many different areas of difficulty, when the Lord answers you in all of them, you will have more to talk about. Your testimony will have more impact, and your faith will be great. With any particular disease that you are suffering from—HIV, cancer, hypertension, diabetes, or any other chronic disease—God is giving you a word of knowledge today, and that word is simply "know that you know!" In other words, firstly, become aware that you know that you are given a word of knowledge. Secondly, know that you will recover and tell people about the power of healing; that's your ministry. Thirdly, know that God is giving you an understanding of greatness by conquering the spirit of infirmities, sickness, and disease so that you testify about what He has done for you and also assist those who are going through the same thing you went through.

Receive that word of knowledge and walk with it. Religious people can't access this truth, because they don't talk to God but they talk to themselves. They don't open a channel from their hearts to download the things that would plead genuinely with the mercies and grace of Christ. They do not activate a lifestyle of serving Christ and acknowledge the power of His spirit. Refrain from being a religious person, and you will be next in line to testify.

Religion has brought the name of our Lord Jesus to a point of disrepute. Those who follow "religion" are not sure if what they do will work or not; they are still trying to figure things out. Rather, use your experience in Christ to become a spiritual commander ... to become a giant in the kingdom of God and to bring the works of the devil to shame.

Galatians 6:1: *"You who are spiritual should restore."*

One effective method of restoration is sharing your testimony. Somebody is waiting to hear what your ears have heard and what your eyes have seen. Somebody is waiting to know how you made something possible. The only way God can cause people to marvel is through your story. See yourself like that. Tell yourself that you shall rise and receive the word of knowledge from the Lord in order to restore others. But do not be deceived; religion will not bring you to that point. Only a continuous intimacy with Christ will usher you into a life as a spiritual commander in the kingdom of Christ.

Colossians 3:23: *"Whatever you do, work heartily, as for the Lord and not for men."*

How does God differentiate between a staunch Christian and a "religious Christian"? By their services. A "religious Christian" does not do things wholeheartedly for God; rather, he does things wholeheartedly for people. He can decide to tend the sheep when others are going for worship. These are people who are in churches, doing church duties not for God but for themselves. They live their lives for religion, not for the Lord. Their lives have turned into a routine that has no direction and is guided by self more than the Spirit of Christ. They will proudly speak of their church with very little of Christ in the picture. They have established buildings as substitutes for the Lord. The question that one may ask is, whom are they serving? And which spirit is guiding them?

One sad thing is that Christ is not in their midst, although they have many reasons mapped out to convince others that the spirit of Christ is working. An individual who wants to show others that Christ is in his or her life has no Christ. Christ cannot be marketed by people. He reveals Himself. Those who try to convince people of the presence of the Lord in their lives end up manipulating, and who is the father of manipulation?

Do not market Christ, but rather allow Christ to market you. There is a vast difference between sharing God's word and marketing Christ. Do not allow the devil to deceive you. You don't need religion, but you need God's spirit … an oracle of grace. The power of His glory gives life and strength to overcome life's challenges.

"Righteous Talk, Unrighteous Practices"

First John 3:7: *"Little children, let no one deceive you. Whoever practices righteousness is righteous, as he [God] is righteous."*

What made John write to God's children about righteous practices? It was the way they were living their lives, especially those who claimed that they had received Christ.

He warned God's children of those who talk righteousness but practice unrighteousness. Other people do not want to commit themselves to Christ, but they call themselves born-again Christians; in fact, there is only one kind of Christian, and that's a born-again Christian—nothing more … nothing less. These people have made it clear to themselves that they will never receive Christ as their Savior, but they will only use His name to deceive all those who follow Christ wholeheartedly. For John to talk about this deception implies that many believers were robbed by many who were among their midst, posing as lovers of truth, but deep in their hearts seeking an opportunity to scatter and lead them astray.

But there is one thing that those vultures forget to do. And that is to sustain their falsified righteous practices. If other people say they have met up with the deceivers who can speak like real Christians, preach and teach like the apostles, heal the sick, do mighty miracles, and even prophesy, then how will you know if you are being deceived?

First John 4:6: *"We are from God. Whoever knows God listens to us; whoever is not from God does not listen to us. By this we know the Spirit of truth and the spirit of error."*

Those who are from God are filled with the spirit of God and the knowledge of His word. They do not speak their words, but they speak God's words as proof of their origin. What comes out of their mouths is fire, for they speak God's words.

Jeremiah 23:29: *"Is not my word like fire."*

It is only when you speak God's word to one another that you will know people's true hearts. Those who carry God's words will be filled up, and those who are deceptive will not stand; they will crumble. They will not be comfortable, and they will not agree with what comes out of your mouth. Speak God's word over men and women of God, in your home, over your children and family, in your office, on your mode of transport, and there is no demon that will stand.

Those who are not from God cannot comprehend or receive these words, because their evil spirits manifest, and the fire of the Lord consumes their works. Therefore, train yourself to be a man or a woman of fire and send it on those who are close to you. Allow them to catch fire, and there is no demon on earth that will stand. Learn to pray for every pastor you know by releasing the fire of the Lord into their lives. False ministers will never ever be able to stand you. There is no demon above or below earth that will be able to stand you, because the words of God are like fire, and through them the spirit of truth and error will be known. When the Bible says that the spirit of error will be known, it means it will be identified, exposed, and revealed, because the spirit of truth will expose its origin, its name, and its purpose. The spirit of truth is the spirit that also reveals lies.

The reason that there are many false prophets who rob people of their possessions from God is that we do not send the word of the Lord directly into their lives to expose their deeds.

Jeremiah 23:15: *"Therefore thus says the Lord of hosts concerning the [false] prophets: 'Behold, I will feed them with bitter food and give them poisoned water to drink.'"*

Demons do not feed on God's word; they feed on lies, greed, immorality, lust, quarrelling, fighting, and hatred. This is what makes them strong and what makes you weak. But when you pronounce the word of the Lord to an evil spirit, the word is poison. This is what makes them weak and what makes you strong—the word of God. Only God's people enjoy God's word. It is only they who will say it is good to eat from God's table. But to the wicked it is bitterness. Haven't you asked yourself why people who don't know Jesus become impatient when you begin to speak the word of God? They become unsettled and uncomfortable. That's the reason. Some begin to have funny thoughts that you think you are better off, and they look around trying connect you to any wrongdoing they know you of, and this is how many resist Christ. All this takes place in their spirit simply because that word was poison to the spirit that rules their lives.

Philippians 4:8: *"Finally, brothers, whatever is true, whatever is honorable, whatever is just, whatever is pure, whatever is lovely, whatever is commendable, if there is any excellence, if there is anything worthy of praise, think about these things."*

Whenever you seek a man or woman of God, seek these things: truth, honour, love, commendableness, excellence, and praise of God.

If you see a "believer" who does not carry these attributes, that is a sign that there is no presence of the Lord operating in his or her life. If it's a person who says he or she is "of God", then why follow?

Why follow a man or a woman who does not praise the Lord but praises the works of his or her own hands ... someone who is not truthful and has no love for the sheep? These are not the qualities of a true believer. Every believer should be a just person full of honour, love, commendableness, and excellence. A true believer looks for these things and strives to attain them. Therefore, we need to learn to acknowledge and appreciate those who are doing their best to be acceptable before the Lord. These are the qualities that the Apostle Paul possessed and wanted others to know how to identify a true believer.

Philippians 4:9: *"What you have learned and received and heard and seen in me—practice these things, and the God of peace will be with you."*

If you practice righteousness in speech and deed, you will see the works of the God of peace in your life. The one who practices righteousness is righteous because He is righteous. When you live a righteous life, you are living the life that God has destined for you. You will live just like God. This means that righteous living is godly living. When you live a godly lifestyle you are representing God, and nothing will be impossible for you to do, because nothing is impossible for God to do. Nothing has stood before God, and nothing shall stand before you. Whatever you put your mind to will be achievable, and whatever you wish to build shall be established. It is not righteous talk that produces such results; rather, it is righteous practices that cause you to operate in such dimensions because God is a doer of righteousness.

Chapter 6

Carrying the Cross

Matthew 10:38: *"And whoever does not take his cross and follow me is not worthy of me."*

Is it really necessary to carry the cross of Jesus? What is the cross for? Does the cross of Jesus really save us from everything He came to set us free from?

Carrying the cross of Christ signifies the ultimate surrender to the true God. It is an act that separates us from our sinful nature of the flesh in order to gain the nature of God. It is a sacrifice. The route of the cross reaches out to give Jesus access and dominion in our lives. It is only through the cross that you receive the freedom of your soul from bondage, signifying the totality of Christ's reign over your being.

Christ suffered so that we might gain everything. If God had not allowed Christ to suffer, there would have been total dominion of evil on earth. The world would have been a place of total darkness where the devil would be king. Christ had to come, and personally encounter evil personalities, characters and attributes possessed by evil men. This was to demonstrate to His children how they can individually demolish, terminate and break loose from the Chains of such evil behaviors projected to hinder their productivity. He did this by showing us how we can overcome evil treatments from others, by simply adhering to His teachings and the practices He displayed, whenever evil personalities from man rises as obstacles to impede our destination. And the only way to bring light and hope to conquer the devil was to personally encounter those evil habits that man had already inherited from the devil by demonstrating to the world how they should imitate Him in overcoming the evil conducts that we display amongst one another. Christ came to show us that, when we surrender our lives to Him, these evil treatments we receive from other people indirectly lead us to our destiny. He came to show us that, in fact, evil treatment you receive from your colleagues, your family members, or society in general is something that can uplift you; it can serve as a corridor to greatness and an escalator to mighty works … a catalyst to success …a facilitator to stability and a pathway to knowing the character of the most high God.

False Witness Exercises Truthfulness

Mark 14:56: *"For many bore false witness against him."*

Christ was falsely accused so that we could gain His truthfulness. A false accusation is an accusation full of lies in an attempt to ruin someone's reputation. Whenever you are falsely accused of something that you did not do, know that the Lord wants to establish you in truthfulness. When people gather and speak lies about you, they are taking you into the dimension of being a truthful person. Christ destroyed the power of lies in order for us to gain what is true.

There has to come a stage in your walk with Christ when you realize that lies spoken by man are a doorway for God to produce in you truthfulness. The devil tried to cause Christ to fall by falsely accusing Him. Little did he know that this kind of a human being was waiting for false witnessing so he could prove to God His truthfulness. Christ was not provoked by the lies that were spoken about Him; rather, He saw them as an opportunity to demonstrate how to crumble the foundations of lies by just seeking the truth. Similarly, when the storm of lies rises against your life, seek the truth.

John 8:42–47: *"Jesus said to them, 'If God were your Father, you would love me, for I came from God and I am here. I came not of my own accord, but he sent me. Why do you not understand what I say? It is because you cannot bear to hear my word. You are of your father the devil, and your will is to do your father's desires. He was a murderer from the beginning, and has nothing to do with the truth, because there is no truth in him. When he lies, he speaks out of his own character, for he is a liar and the father of lies. But because I tell the truth, you do not believe me. Which one of you convicts me of sin? If I tell the truth, why do you not believe me? Whoever is of God hears the words of God. The reason why you do not hear them is that you are not of God.'"*

The devil is the father of lies. He has been lying from the beginning. And there is no truth in him. Christ could not compromise His truthfulness because of the lies of the devil because He knew where He came from.

People who strive to give false witnesses about you are not from God. In them there is no truth, and God is not their father. Nothing that they do is truth, for they speak out of their own character. It does not matter who is in the group of those who lie about you. It can be your employer trying to pull you down, or a member of your family or church. Just be truthful to your Father by been loyal.

John 8:31–32: *"So Jesus said to the Jews who had believed in him, 'If you abide in my word, you are truly my disciple, and you will know the truth, and the truth will set you free.'"*

The truth is not in everyone, but it is in those who abide in Christ. These are the ones who abide in His word. Is there a plot against your life? Are you falsely accused? Has your family given false witness against you? Look for Christ. Look for Him in His word.

John 8:34–36: *"Truly, truly, I say to you, everyone who commits sin is a slave to sin. The slave does not remain in the house forever; the son remains forever. So if the Son sets you free, you will be free indeed."*

This qualifies our Lord Jesus Christ to be the only source of truth …the one who has the authority to set us free from lies and false witnessing rose against our lives. If Christ could have forsaken the truth for lies, we all could have been won over by the devil. But He understood that truly, truly, lies are a sin, and everyone who commits sin is a slave to sin. This means that when you live a truthful life, you do not commit sin and you are free. Whenever you are been falsely accused, rejoice, for the Lord is granting you the truth of Christ. Truthful people are tested by false witnesses. Do not sort out what is false to retaliate; rather, praise God, for He is establishing you in His truthfulness.

Matthew 5:33–36: *"Again you have heard that it was said to those of old, 'You shall not swear falsely, but shall perform to the Lord what you have sworn.' But I say to you, Do not take an oath at all, either by heaven, for it is the throne of God, or by the earth, for it is his footstool, or by Jerusalem, for it is the city of the great King."*

What makes truthfulness one of the major attributes that a believer should aspire to have? An oath is a promise and a vow that one makes in a statement to someone. God is not pleased with false vows. A false vow is a promise that you are not intending to keep. When God plans our future, our vows are very important. They represent our commitment to Him, and they encourage Him to decide matters in our favor. That is why people who keep their promises to God succeed, and those who fail to keep them receive a penalty. Christ told us not to make an oath at all if we know that we are not going to honor it.

And if you make an oath and you fail to keep it, repent, in order to set yourself free from God's penalty. The devil even deceives people to make vows that they know they will not keep. They lie to God. The devil leads them to commit an offence that will make them receive nothing from the Lord. This makes God know who your true father is. Truthfulness is one of the fundamental tools a believer can use to conquer evil. In order for that truthfulness to be affirmed, false witnesses will rise, and it is only the truth you get from Christ that will defend you against false accusers. Truthfulness is an act of worship to the Lord.

John 4:22–23: *"You worship what you do not know; we worship what we know ... But the hour is coming, and is now here, when the true worshipers will worship the Father in spirit and truth, for the Father is seeking such people to worship Him."*

The Father is on a mission to seek those who will worship Him in truth. Worship in songs is not key to truthfulness, but maintaining the knowledge of Christ in your heart in your day-to-day living establishes a truthful worship in everything you do. Then what do you think will run parallel to allow God to witness whether you are truthful or not? Definitely, false accusations. They are very relevant for evaluating the capacity of your truthfulness to Christ. The principle of maintaining the truth when everyone believes it will pull you down is what God wants to see in you. One thing that we must know is that the Father will not allow Himself to be worshiped by lies. To satisfy Him, you should remain rooted in His truth under all circumstances.

It is the truthful worshipers who will lead the church into an acceptable worship—not the gifted worshipers. You can be gifted with the ability to sing, but not be truthful. God is looking for people who will understand whom He is, what can He do, and what He wants. A worshipper must carry himself or herself in a truthful manner in order to move God.

Allow your accusers to give a false witness against you. Allow them to discuss and speak lies about you amongst people who might be able to influence your destination. Do not be discouraged by their ways of thinking toward you; rather, look at it as a platform God can use to raise you into His truthfulness, because He is intending to use you to reveal the truth. Once you have stood and borne all the false testimonies your accusers have given against you, begin to thank the Lord for seeking and finding you. Thank Him for using your accusers as a ladder to truthfulness. Thank Him for searching your heart in the midst of lies, and once you are convinced that you are truthful, begin to worship Him. Worship Him in truth, and you will capture His heart. It is not the gifted who move God, but the truthful.

It is in that worship that the chains of evil pronounced against your life will be crumbled, and the plans of darkness exposed. It is in that worship that the name of our Lord Jesus will be glorified and the devil put to shame. Do not stand there and ask yourself why they are bringing up stories about your life; rather, praise God for locating you. Praise Him for seeking you among the rest, and praise Him for granting you the opportunity to exercise truthfulness.

Second Corinthians 13:8: *"For we cannot do anything against the truth."*

There is no arrow that will strike you when you are established in the truth, and no witch can do anything against your destiny when you have tied truthfulness around your waist. They can absolutely do nothing against you when you are a truthful person.

Humiliated to Exercise Humility

Acts 8:33: *"In his [Jesus's] humiliation justice was denied him."*

The humiliation of Christ was a doorway for us to acquire humility. When Christ was humiliated, His judgment was taken away (KJV). Does this mean that He could no longer judge? No, but this means that the act of His humiliation brought Him to a state that brought out His humility. When Christ was humiliated on His way to the cross, He was very humble; He did not exercise His ability to judge. He became a king who did not exercise His ability to judge when He was put to shame. With all the right to strike back at His accusers and with all the understanding to reason out His innocence, He decided to allow His ability to judge to be put aside. And not only that, He allowed it to be taken away from Him. What this means is that God did not take away the judgment of Christ, but Christ lowered Himself to the extent of ignoring His capacity to judge. The ability to judge was still within Him, but He did not use it; hence, the Bible says it was taken away. He was the same Christ who had done good throughout His lifetime. He did not change, and He also did not intend to change. What you have to understand is that, when He was humiliated on His way to the cross, He allowed His ability to judge to become inactive and dormant. He allowed it to be of no use to Him, even allowing Himself to appear to be a person who could not utter a word of judgment. He did not challenge the evidence that was brought against Him. He did not talk back to them, and He did not try to show them that they had got the wrong person. He just substituted His humiliation with humility—humility before God and before His accusers. His humiliation became a platform that enabled Him to be humble. When they were thinking of how best they could humiliate Him, He thought of how best He could humble Himself. He became submissive to those who humiliated Him.

Hosea 3:1–3: *"And the Lord said to me, 'Go again, love a woman who is loved by another man and is an adulterous, even as the Lord loves the children of Israel, though they turn to other gods and love cakes of raisins.' So I bought her for fifteen shekels of silver and a homer and a lethech of barley. And I said to her, "You must dwell as mine for many days."'*

If Hosea had not allowed himself to be humiliated by God's command, the Lord could have not used him as vessel to convey a message to the children of Israel for them to see how they had sinned against the Lord. Hosea chose to be humiliated rather than to compromise his humility and obedience toward the Lord. His humiliation was a doorway through which the world could see his submissiveness to God despite unpleasant circumstances. Also, Hosea's ability to judge was taken away from him. He did not complain to the Lord, but he obeyed. His status in society did not matter, but he chose the way that the Lord had destined for him. Humiliation provokes, degrades, and leaves one without any reputation. It embarrasses you and takes away your pride as a person, especially if you are a prophet and the Lord commanded you to marry a woman loved by many men—an adulterous.

Proverbs 29:23: *"One's pride will bring him low, but he who is lowly in spirit will obtain honor."*

Who are the people who make it when they are humiliated and yet remain humble? The lowly in spirit.

Matthew 5:3: *"Blessed are the poor in spirit, for theirs is the kingdom of heaven."*

When you are humiliated and yet become humble, the doors of the kingdom of God are opened to you. The kingdom of God is a kingdom of the lowly and the poor, for they are the ones God has chosen to walk by faith.

James 2:5: *"Listen, my beloved brothers, has not God chosen those who are poor in the world to be rich in faith and heirs of the kingdom."*

The rich take one another to court, because they want to redeem their pride. But the poor walk by faith, and God has given them the blessing to inherit His kingdom. There is no other way to become an heir in God's kingdom besides being humble and lowly in spirit, and this is justified by your actions when you are humiliated. The grace of God will be shown whenever you become humble.

James 4:6: *"God opposes the proud, but gives grace to the humble."*

Who are the proud? They are those who fight their battles when they are humiliated. Humiliation triggers pride and temper, and this the Lord opposes. Your pride is aroused when you are wronged and nobody comes to ask for forgiveness. Refuse to allow your pride to manifest by retaliating, because God will oppose your actions as well; rather, seek to become humble. Pray to God to grant you that special grace in order to let it all go. Sometimes we become like our enemies when we attempt to rescue our pride, yet we are all born without it.

First John 2:16: *"For all that is in the world—the desires of the flesh and the desires of the eyes and pride in possessions—is not from the Father but is from the world."*

Are you seeking an opportunity to redeem your pride? Are you having sleepless nights trying to figure out how you can repay those who humiliated you? Are you undermined by those you lead? Has your partner humiliated you in public? Then there is only one thing that you should know, and that is that you are dealing with the foundations of your pride. Ask God to grant you a lowly spirit and thank Him for the platform He has set that you can use to understand the capacity of your humility. Allow your desire to judge to be taken away from you. Do not fight back or talk back at them, for your pride will be taking the place of God to defend you, and God will oppose you as well. Simply, just leave it all in the hands of the Lord. It is not your pride that matters when you are humiliated, but it is your humility that should not be compromised. Christ was humiliated in order that we could gain His humility. Believers have no choice but to stay humble under all circumstances. When we humble ourselves, we live up to what Christ did on His way to the cross, and the grace of God seeks those who walk according to the standards and principles of the Lord. Do not see humiliation as a weapon, but look at it as an elevator you can use to access the blessings of the Lord.

Hated to Love

John 15:18: *"If the world hates you, know that it has hated me before it hated you."*

Jesus prepared His disciples against the hatred they would receive on earth. And this is the reason:

John 15:19: *"If you were of the world, the world would love you as its own; but because you are not of the world, but I chose you out of the world, therefore the world hates you."*

These reasons are enough to explain why we will be hated by the world, but we will need a deeper understanding to comprehend it and to make it a way of life. Christ came to set people free from bondage. Hence, the one who is binding people is displeased and angry toward those who are being set free as well as toward the one who set them free. Christ was led to the cross by hatred, and yet the cross became His victory. This shows you how hatred of the world can become an important attribute in shaping you to become a glorious and victorious ambassador of Christ. When the principalities of the kingdom of darkness came on Him, He allowed Himself to be driven by them into greatness, for they hated Him without a cause.

John 15:25: *"But the word that is written in their Law must be, fulfilled: "They hated me without a cause.""*

Are you hated without a cause? Then do not be dismayed. Most believers wonder why people hate them. You will have a person confessing with his own mouth saying, "My dear brother, I can't hide it any longer. You know I hate you." When you try to figure out why this person is speaking like that, you can't see the reason. Do not beat yourself up by analyzing such confessions, but this is what you will experience. Know that you will be hated without a cause. No matter how hard you try to convince them, their minds are captivated, and there is nothing you can do to make them love you.

Second Samuel 13:6–17: *"So Amnon lay down and pretended to be ill. And when the king came to see him, Amnon said to the king, 'Please let my sister Tamar come and make a couple of cakes in my sight, that I may eat from her hand.' Then David sent home to Tamar, saying, 'Go to your brother Amnon's house and prepare food for him.' So Tamar went to her brother Amnon's house, where he was lying down. And she took dough and kneaded it and made cakes in his sight and baked the cakes. And she took the pan and emptied it out before him, but he refused to eat. And Amnon said, 'Send out everyone from me.' So everyone went out from him. Then Amnon said to Tamar, 'Bring the food into the chamber, that I may eat from your hand.' And Tamar took the cakes she had made and brought them into the chamber to Amnon her brother. But when she brought them near him to eat, he took hold of her and said to her, 'Come, lie with me, my sister.' She answered him, 'No, my brother, do not violate me, for such a thing is not done in Israel; do not do this outrageous thing. As for me, where could I carry my shame? And as for you, you would be as one of the outrageous fools in Israel. Now therefore, please speak to the king, for he will not withhold me from you.' But he would not listen to her, and being stronger than she, he violated her and lay with her. Then Amnon hated her with very great hatred, so that the hatred with which he hated her was greater than the love with which he had loved her. And Amnon said to her, 'Get up! Go!' But she said to him, 'No, my brother, for this wrong in sending me away is greater than the other that you did to me.' But he would not listen to her. He called the young man who served him and said, 'Put this woman out of my presence and bolt the door after her.'"*

Three times did Tamar perform the requests made by Amnon, and not even once did Amnon listen to her requests. Her requests were all void to him. She did her utmost best to satisfy Amnon and do whatever it took to make sure that her relationship with her brother was intact. In fact, she also suggested to Amnon that she did not mind being committed to him, but only if the king were informed about their affair, but that request also was in vain. Despite all her attempts to satisfy him, Amnon never listened to her, and he violated her and lay with her by force.

The love that he had once had for her changed into hatred. He even did a more outrageous thing by chasing her away. Even after Tamar suggested to him that sending her away was a greater offence, still Amnon chased her away. And he did not even make any proposal to marry her; this is what broke her into pieces. After preserving herself, this is the reward she got. She had not lain with any man, and the first time she did was in an outrageous manner. And to make it all worse, that man was her brother, who was no more interested in her, and he then even developed a great hatred of her. Amnon definitely hated her without cause.

Life can sometimes treat you in the same way that Amnon treated Tamar. After doing whatever it takes to put everything in place for your manager, what he gives back is an outrageous violation of your rights.

In that same mood you will see hatred develop to be greater than the love a person offered you before finishing with you. Tamar prepared dough, which must rise before it is baked. The dough, before it rises, represents the love that was offered. And the dough, after it has risen, represents the hatred that followed. Dough increases in size as it rises. This means that sometimes we should not be excited about a sudden rise of love from nowhere that a person offers us. Either that person wants you to do something for him, or he wants you. Amnon commanded his young men to carry his sister out of his presence and fasten the door behind her, meaning that he did not even want to give her a chance of coming back to him. No matter how hard she would try, the hatred against her had taken over.

Tamar was prepared to learn how to love him only if he did not send her away. She tried to hide Amnon's evil acts by making him aware that she was a woman of principle, and only if she talked to the king would all be well for them. Look how far Tamar went in trying to satisfy Amnon. She had every right to hate her brother, but instead it was Amnon the violator who hatred her more than she hated him. This is how truly evil the devil is. People may cause you pain and make your life desolate, and also show no remorse for their actions. Such practices are common to those you have opened your heart to and assisted through their fake schemes.

Song of Solomon 8:7: *"Many waters cannot quench love, neither can floods drown it."*

Hatred is a flood; its sole mission is to destroy love. But *"many waters cannot quench love."*

When you accept Jesus as your personal Savior, you open a door of love, and only the hatred in this world will challenge the capacity of the love you have for Him. If you are hated by the whole world for no reason, then you have a love that is greater than that of the whole world. And if you are loved by the world and hated by an individual, the love you have is questionable. No amount of water can quench love. When ultimately your love is quenched, then its foundation is questionable, for the Bible say many waters cannot quench love. But those who have sought the true love of God will prevail against floods. They shall stand when the hatred of multitudes rises against them, and they shall withstand days of evil. The ability to forgive, reconcile, and forget evil that is done to you indicates the capacity of the true love of Christ you carry.

Second Corinthians 5:17–18: *"Therefore, if anyone is in Christ, he is a new creation. The old has passed away; behold, the new has come. All this is from God, who through Christ reconciled us to himself and gave us the ministry of reconciliation."*

In other words, in Christ, God was reconciling the world to Himself, not counting their trespasses against them and entrusting to us the message of reconciliation.

Some people wonder if they are still a new creation because they have been in the Lord for a long period of time. Absolutely. What you should understand is that, whenever you are in Christ, you continue to be a new creation all the days of your life. You are new the day you receive Christ, and you are still new and you will always be a new creation.

Since you are new, you have received the ministry and then the message of reconciliation. Also, become aware of the order in which the Apostle Paul mentions these services of reconciliation. Why does he mention the ministry of reconciliation before the message? Is it not the message then the ministry? Well in this instance it is not like that. Because the ministry of reconciliation is nowhere but in Christ. You have to be in Him to receive that ministry before you can speak of its message. It is not appropriate to speak the message of the reconciler before you encounter Him. This means that, if you reconcile with a person outside of Christ and you don't want to be in Him, your actions will all be in vain.

The ministry of reconciliation and its message display to the world the character of God that they do not know. Its main objective is to bring people together to live in the grace of our Lord Jesus Christ. You cannot walk with someone unless you reconcile together; similarly, you cannot walk with God unless you reconcile with Him through His son Jesus Christ.

The spirit of hatred is a terminator spirit. It can cause great harm in your life when it is practiced by people who are against your life or if you practice it against other people. And if you are not prepared to follow the teachings of the Holy Spirit, your life will become a tragedy. They hated Christ first before they hated you, and they hate you because you are of the light. Nevertheless, always be ready to practice the ministry and the message of reconciliation.

John 1:9–10: *"The true light which enlightens everyone, was coming into the world. He was in the world, and the world was made through him, yet the world did not know him."*

Hatred does not know love, and darkness does not know light. And those who hate you don't know you, and those who are in darkness can't appreciate your light. Therefore, have this mentality—that those who live in darkness cannot comprehend your ways. They can't understand your ways and your actions, and thus they are swallowed by wickedness. Also understand that love directs hate, and light directs darkness, and love is supreme to hate. Those who hate you will never understand you unless they come to the light and bear that love that you carry. Only then will they begin to understand and know who you are.

Rejected, Isolated, and Bound to Be Free

Isaiah 53:3: *"He was … rejected by men; a man of sorrows, and acquainted with grief."*

Isaiah prophesied the life of Christ long before He was born. What Isaiah spoke and wrote about was not accepted and understood by those who lived at that time. This is evident by the introduction he made in the opening verse of Isaiah 53:

Isaiah 53:1: *"Who has believed what they heard from us? And to whom has the arm of the Lord been revealed?"*

Isaiah proclaimed that, for the people to believe his prophecy, only the arm of the Lord needs to be revealed. His prophecy was that Christ would be rejected by men. To the people there, this prophecy did not make sense. They heard it, but they did not understand it. The Messiah will not be accepted by men? How? Why? He will be rejected and many will not believe in him? In Isaiah's time nobody could comprehend this prophecy, and probably they began to doubt the God of Isaiah's prophecies. Even today, many still don't believe that Jesus was really the Messiah.

We all at some point in our lives have rejected Christ by refusing to believe in His words. No man can claim he knew Christ before He come into his life. And no man can know Christ except He allows him to know who He is.

This causes those who don't understand its operations to reject the ministry of Christ. But why did God allow Christ to be sent to earth if He knew that He would be rejected? If God could have kept Christ in heaven away from those who would reject Him, His Kingdom could have forfeited the mandate to set man free from bondage. Why? Because Christ gave us our freedom, and through Him came love, grace, life and light.

Ephesians 2:3–4: *"For by grace you have been saved through faith. And this is not your own doing; it is the gift of God, not a result of works, so that no one may boast."*

This made it the responsibility of God to save us through His son Jesus Christ, not through our deeds. Christians are also in this world to minister salvation of He who came to set man free.

John 1:12–13: *"But to all who did receive him, who believed in his name, he gave the right to become children of God, who were born, not of blood nor of the will of the flesh nor of the will of man, but of God."*

Just as the prophecy of Isaiah stated, only the arm of God is able to reveal Christ in our lives to the world that rejected Him. But those who accepted Christ when He revealed Himself to them qualify to be the children of God and are set free from all forms of bondage from the kingdom of darkness.

Matthew 26:42–44: *"Again, for the second time, he went away and prayed, 'My Father, if this cannot pass unless I drink it, your will be done.' And again he came and found them sleeping, for their eyes were heavy. So, leaving them again, he went away and prayed for the third time, saying the same words again."*

When the people you expected to be there in times of difficulty fail you and refuse to go that extra mile with you, do not anticipate failure. Isolation by people is sometimes more evident in actions than it is in words. And when Christ was isolated from His disciples, He refused to be demoralized; rather, He took advantage of that separation to seek His God. That isolation created a door for Him through which He could be more intimate with God. It became a platform from which He could have an encounter with His God.

Similarly, when the people you thought would be your pillar reject or become isolated from you, that situation is just a challenge for you to close the door and find a secluded corner where you will meet with your Maker. It is an opportunity to study God's word and to pray. Just look at it this way—if Jesus was accepted and loved by all, and earth would have been a pleasant place for Him to be, that would have lead Him to compromise His mission here on earth.

Are you rejected, isolated, and bound? Seek God, for He does not isolate you or reject you. The more you are rejected by man, the more time you have to you to worship your God. Go to any church that believes in Jesus and ask truthful intercessors the reason they are so dedicated in prayer. One of the reasons they will give to you is that man has rejected them and they felt isolated, but Christ accepted them into fellowship with the spirit of God.

Thank God for people who don't want to be with you. Glorify the Lord when your best friend decides you are no longer his choice. Glorify God when that person you trusted with your family felt that other people were better than you are. Look, if a man or a woman leaves you, she or he is leaving you in the hands of the Lord. And if at work they have decided to make you redundant, praise God, for now you will have time with Christ. And who has ever failed after coming out of seclusion with the Holy Spirit? Who has been depressed after spending an immeasurable length of time with His God? If you fail after diligently calling to God for His intervention over your life, know that you will be the first one to experience that, for in God there is no failure nor limitations.

Acts 26:19–23: *"Therefore, O King Agrippa, I was not disobedient to the heavenly vision, but declared first to those in Damascus, then in Jerusalem and throughout all the region of Judea, and also to the Gentiles, that they should repent and turn to God, performing deeds in keeping with their repentance. For this reason the Jews seized me in the temple and tried to kill me. To this day I have had the help that comes from God, and so I stand here testifying both to small and great, saying nothing but what the prophets and Moses said would come to pass: that the Christ must suffer and that, by being the first to rise from the dead, he would proclaim light both to our people and to the Gentiles."*

And as he was saying these things in his defense, Festus told Paul with a loud voice that Paul was out of his mind ... his great learning was driving him out of his mind (Acts 26:24).

Today everyone who calls himself or herself a Christian leans on the teachings and the ministry of Christ through the Apostle Paul. But in his time, people like Festus did not accept him. Now make your own analysis. Of Paul and Festus, which one was out of his mind? Paul said that, until that day, he had experienced the help that came from God, so he would stand there to testify. Which platform do you see yourself testifying from after the Lord has made a way for you? It is good advice to seek a platform that has both the small and the great in it. When you minister to people on the major elevation the Lord will bring to you, many will begin to associate you with insanity. To those who isolated themselves from you, such words will be words of madness, because they will have thought nobody would see anything good in you. Yes, they were right. Nobody will see anything good in you—but God will.

It was the Apostle Paul's testimony of the Lord, when Paul was on his way to Damascus, that set him free from spiritual bondage. Even though he spent most of his ministry rejected and bound in chains, spiritually he was free, and the heavens had accepted him. This is what matters. When you try your utmost best to please the Lord and minister salvation to people, they look at you and see a person who is out of his mind. Praise be to God, because if it's your own mind you are using and not that of the

Spirit of God, you are still in bondage, so you have to be out of it in order to function with the spirit.

Acts 26:32: *"And Agrippa said to Festus, 'This man could have been set free if he had not appealed to Caesar.'"*

When they are physically bound in chains and rejected, it is tempting for most people to say they are not free. They assess freedom by what they see in you.

Most people in leadership positions in institutions assume that they have the keys of their sub-ordinate in their hands, not knowing that their mentality is serious deception from the kingdom of darkness. When they reject your deservedly merits; awards you rightfully qualify for. Little do they know that you are free in spirit, and they are the ones who are bound spiritually by their wickedness.

Paul was not out of his mind when he ministered Christ, because he did not mind ministering about Him; he was free and accepted by God. Whenever you are cast out by family, friends, and society, rejoice, for the Lord is near. Your intimacy with Him will prove its meaning in days of trouble. Your relationship with Christ is strengthened by those who did not want you amongst them, and the stability of that relationship is proven when you come out of seclusion.

Isaiah 40:31: *"But they who wait for the Lord shall renew their strength; they shall mount up with wings like eagles; they shall run and not be weary; they shall walk and not faint."*

Every time you enter His presence, your strength will be renewed, your purpose in life will be reaffirmed, and your desires will be accelerated into existence. Yes, some will continue to see you as that person they rejected … that brother living in chains …living in financial chains. But in you will be hidden a treasure of purpose, a stream of many waters, and the light of life that is waiting to come into existence.

Wait in the Lord. Wait, for He is near. When He has finally arrived, it will be evident, as the psalmist wrote in Psalm 57:6: *"They dug a pit in my way, but they have fallen into it themselves."*

Their expectations will fall in their own pit. That's not your pit, but it's their pit, the one designed for you. It is that pit into which their feet will fall.

The Lord will carry you.

Rejection is a red carpet to divinity. Being in the Lord ushers the small to greatness, builds the low to the highest height, and sharpens the spirit and the mind, preparing you for more exploits.

Mocked To Have Patience

Luke 23:11–12: *"And Herod with his soldiers treated him with contempt and mocked him. Then, carrying him in splendid clothing, he sent him back to Pilate. And Herod and Pilate became friends with each other that very day, for before this they had been at enmity with each other."*

The day that Jesus was mocked was the day that a new friendship between two people who were enemies began. Herod and Pilate, who had been lifetime enemies, now had something to talk about. Christ became the good news they told one another, and His silence and their mockery of Him became a topic to be enjoyed between them.

Are you aware that sometimes people who have known each other but have not been on good terms with one another find it possible to establish their friendship by making fun and ridiculing other people? Mockery is a strategy used by the devil to shift your attention from the vision you are intending to achieve. Christ could easily have responded when the soldiers mocked Him, but He chose to remain silent. Imagine if the soldiers could have managed to anger Him; they could have led Him to sin, disqualifying Him as a sacrifice without blemish. But to Him silence brought patience. Being silent is not a sign of defeat; it is a sign that you are adhering surely to your purpose, steadfastly enduring with patience.

Acts 17:32: *"Now when they heard of the resurrection of the dead, some mocked."*

Paul was ministering about the resurrection of the dead, and some mocked. They mocked the truth and the power of God, and they ridiculed God. Now, people who mock the gospel show how limited they are, because they mock what is true and advanced.

Do you want to know whether you are advancing or not? Then look around and you will see people mocking the decisions you make, mocking your contributions you are making in life and mocking what the Lord has commanded you to do. It is painful to God when a believer mocks another believer or a church of Christ mocks another church of God.

If people begin to mock you, know that you should take the opportunity to exercise your patience. You can preach the gospel of God with patience by ignoring some statements that will pull you down from God. It is the patience you portray when you are mocked that will sometimes minister to others and ultimately inspire them to walk and talk like you do.

Psalm 89:49–51: *"Lord, where is your steadfast love of old, which by your faithfulness you swore to David? Remember, O Lord, how your servants are mocked, and how I bear in my heart the insults of all the many nations, with which your enemies mock, O Lord, with which they mock the footsteps of your anointed."*

Are you the Lord's servant who is bearing the insults of many people and being mocked by your enemies? Rejoice! For you are the anointed one. The psalmist reveals to us how the footsteps of God's anointed are being mocked. An interesting thing is that the psalmist understood that God's servants are mocked, but he does not see the people who mocked these servants as his enemies; rather, he sees them as God's enemies. This means that whoever mocks the anointed of God becomes the enemy of the Lord.

If you are anointed by the Lord, serving the Lord with your gifts, and there are those who mock what you are doing, take your eyes off them and focus on your call, for those people are not your enemies, but the Lord's.

Look, you are anointed. That is what matters. You are God's chosen servant. You carry the power in you to break every yoke. Don't allow the devil to shift your focus. Just be patient with them, and they will receive their rightful reward from God. Act like Jesus. He became silent. On the other hand, Paul walked out of their midst (Acts 17:33). These were two separate incidents involving two great men of the Kingdom—Jesus and Paul. Both of them were mocked, and neither of them responded. When Jesus was led to the cross and mocked by the soldiers, He remained silent. And when Paul was telling people about the resurrection of the dead, they mocked him also, and he just walked away. The results of the actions of these two men were astounding. Jesus was glorified, and Paul was followed by many men. It is interesting to realize that Paul did not ask anyone to follow him; many saw his conduct and purposed in their hearts to follow him.

Galatians 6:7: *"Do not be deceived: God is not mocked, for whatever one sows, that will he also reap."*

Your patience in God allows Him to be patient with your mockers, and His patience does not mean that He has forsaken you.

Exodus 34:6–7: *"The Lord passed before him and proclaimed, 'The Lord, the Lord a God merciful and gracious, slow to anger, and abounding in steadfast love and faithfulness, keeping steadfast love for thousands, forgiving iniquity and transgression and sin, but who will by no means clear the guilty, visiting the iniquity of the fathers on the children and the children's children, to the third and the fourth generation.'"*

Whenever you bear insults, you bear them in the capacity of God's servant. And whenever people sow evil into your life, it is not your role to visit their iniquity; rather, it is God who does so. We should come to a point where we are as patient as God—slow to anger and abounding in steadfast love.

Luke 23:36: *"The soldiers also mocked him coming up and offering him sour wine."*

Soldier enforces the law and carry out justice in a nation; they are the highest in command in defense of the nation. When Christ came to earth, He brought with Him a kingdom that did not rely on soldiers carrying weapons made by men. But He came to raise spiritual soldiers who would fight spiritual battles rather than physical ones. But the manner in which these earthly soldiers treated Jesus was a sign of how mentally weak they were; they were too weak to guarantee your destiny. Christ exposed the corruption and wickedness that was in their hearts. Rather than leading in the way of justice, they became the way to destruction for many. Their commanders lived in darkness, and they themselves needed a spiritual and godly intervention. Human law failed Him, and He was given sour treatment by the people in highest authority, who lacked spiritual insight.

Some innocent people go to the highest offices to ask for resolution of their matters, and the treatment they receive there, leaves them with a sour taste of life's treatment. Instead of receiving their compensation, they are judged and convicted and thrown away into the streets. Whenever you experience that, rejoice and be patient, for the one who fights and has conquered all spiritual battles is on your side. Be not dismayed, for so the world has done to Him, and it will do the same to you. At the right time, your light will shine. God will use the very same people to uplift you. The very same soldiers, who mocked Jesus, were the same soldiers who lifted him up on the cross. Be patient. Just as they wrote "The King of the Jews" on the cross of Jesus, thinking they were mocking Him and not knowing that indeed He is King, so shall your name be written on the doors of higher places. They will think they are mocking you when they say to you "our manager", "our minister", "our president" or "our prophet" not knowing that so shall the Lord make their words true. Prepare yourself and do not complain. Be silent and accept whatever they offer you, for God is on your side. Look, God is not the respecter of persons (Act 10:34).

If your conscience is clear, He has no choice but to come to your help. Call on Him. He does not show partiality, (Acts 10:34). He will never allow you to fall or to be moved, and He will sustain you. Cast your burden on Him (Psalm 55:22), the perfect and righteous judge (Psalm 9:4)

Betrayed To Be Faithful and Loyal

Mark 14:18–21: *"And as they were reclining at table and eating, Jesus said, 'Truly, I say to you, one of you will betray me, one who is eating with me … one who is dipping bread into the dish with me' … But woe to that man by whom the Son of Man is betrayed! It would have been better for that man if he had not been born."*

What would the world be like if Jesus Christ had betrayed His father? Would God end the world just there, or would have He left it in the hands of the kingdom of darkness? The faithfulness of Christ definitely brought glory to God. His loyalty was tested on many occasions, and He claimed His victory in all of them. Christ had all the opportunity on earth to betray God. He was in human form, and the flesh also demanded something from Him. But in all that He submitted to God's authority and continued to humble Himself.

Philippians 2:8–11: *"And being found in human form, he humbled himself by becoming obedient to the point of death, even death on a cross. Therefore God has highly exalted him and bestowed on him the name that is above every name, so that at the name of Jesus every knee should bow, in heaven and on earth and under the earth, and every tongue confess that Jesus Christ is Lord, to the glory of God the Father."*

This is the attribute that was lacking in the life of Judas—loyalty. He became unfaithful where it mattered most. He allowed the devil to use him to "set Christ up." Yes! *Set Christ Up!* Whenever a person sets you up, it means he takes you high. He prepares seats for you in higher places. Loyalty and faithfulness are recipes for divine success. They are like gas tanks; and, on the other hand, betrayal is like a matchstick. Everytime you are set up, you are being prepared to experience blast … to be the target of a serious explosion that will make a very loud noise and a very huge fire. This makes betrayal an advancer of the promotion of saints. It cultivates and prepares the fields for a greater harvest.

Second Samuel 20:8–10: *"When they were at the great stone that is in Gibeon, Amasa came to meet them. Now Joab was wearing a soldier's garment, and over it was a belt with a sword in it sheath fastened on his thigh, and as he went forward it fell out. And Joab said to Amasa, 'Is it well with you, my brother?' And Joab took Amasa by the beard with his right hand to kiss him. But Amasa did not observe the sword that was in Joab's hand. So Joab struck him with it in the stomach."*

Joab had fully intended to kill Amasa, but Amasa was not aware of it. Even after the sword fell before him, he did not see it as a weapon that would end his life. If he had been vigilant, he could have seen that as a sign of a plot to kill him. But because he thought nothing of Joab, he continued to relax in the presence of his murderer. Sometimes in life, God will show you the weapon that will end your career. It will appear before your eyes, but still you will think nothing of it. This is because of the trust that you have toward individuals who have planned to destroy you.

Jesus knew who would sell Him to the kingdom of darkness, and He knew how and when that evil would occur. This is because of the faithfulness and loyalty He offered to God, and in return God revealed everything to Him. Now this is your mandate—to be loyal to God, and God will be loyal to you when man plots evil against your life. You will not miss your attackers like Amasa, but you shall see them. Special gifts will be given to you to help you see those who plot to bring your life to an end, and He will strengthen you. The sword that is intended to strike you will fall on the ground. That evil from witches shall not touch you or your family members, but shall fall to the ground. Hence, loyalty and faithfulness to God attract favor and reveal every plot of wickedness against your life.

The best time for God to determine whether you are faithful or not is when you are betrayed. Betrayal threatens your faithfulness to God. The moment you decide to take matters into your own hands, you have begun to limit the chances of God defending you. Trusting in God is a sign of faith, and faith is bred by loyalty. No man walks by faith to God without being loyal to Him. The moment you think that you walk by faith with God and you are not loyal to God, then you are not walking with God. The Bible says faith pleases God. It is by faith that God is pleased by those who are faithful. God is not pleased by an unfaithful believer.

First Kings 11:4–8: *"For when Solomon was old his wives turned away his heart after other gods, and his heart was not wholly true to the Lord his God, as was the heart of David his father. For Solomon went after Ashtoreth the goddess of the Sidonians, and after Milcom the abomination of the Ammonites. So Solomon did what was evil in the sight of the Lord and did not wholly follow the Lord, as David his father had done. Then Solomon built a high place for Chemosh the abomination of Moab, and for Molech the abomination of the Ammonites, on the mountain east of Jerusalem. And so he did for all his foreign wives, who made offerings and sacrificed to their gods."*

When God asked Solomon what he wanted, he said wisdom.

First Kings 3:9: *"Give your servant therefore an understanding mind to govern your people, that I may discern between good and evil."*

God fulfilled the request of Solomon to give him wisdom, that he might discern between good and evil. God did according to His word 1 Kings 3:12, and He added riches.

But there was one important attribute that Solomon thought he could cope without, and that was becoming faithful and loyal. Solomon was known all over the world as a very wise man. And he was also known all over the world as an unfaithful man. Today we study his life as one who betrayed the Lord for other gods. He turned his kingdom into a kingdom of idol worship rather than one that worshipped the true God of Israel.

A loyal person has the spirit to discern between evil and good because that's what makes him loyal. A faithful person knows how to walk in truth better than a wise man. Wisdom is not loyalty, but loyalty is wisdom. In other words Solomon could have asked for loyalty which has in it wisdom rather than asking for wisdom which does not have loyalty in it. The same God who was betrayed by Solomon remained faithful to Israel.

First Kings 11:11–13: *"Therefore the Lord said to Solomon, 'Since this has been your practice and you have not kept my covenant and my statutes that I have commanded you, I will surely tear the kingdom from you and will give it to your servant. Yet for the sake of David your father I will not do it in your days, but I will tear it out of the hand of your son. However, I will not tear away all the kingdom, but I will give one tribe to your son, for the sake of David my servant and for the sake of Jerusalem that I have chosen.'"*

Betrayal from man against your life opposes your faithfulness and your loyalty. Solomon was also betrayed by his wives. They knew he served a living God; that's why they married him. But later they turned against him. God is forever faithful, and so must we be. Turn not your back against Him, and He will remain faithful to His promises. For the sake of David, Israel was rescued. Ask God for faithfulness, because this is who He is—faithful. His promises are true. He is not man; He does not lie. Seek His promises from His word and believe them, for He is not a liar.

Titus 3:7 tells us that we are *"justified by his grace so that we might become heirs,"* So shall it be. God is not like man; He does not forsake His children, and all that He spoke concerning your life will come to pass, because He is a faithful God.

Beaten, Pierced, and Wounded to Inherit Peace and Healing

Luke 22:63: *"Now the men who were holding Jesus in custody were mocking him as they beat him."*

The beating of Christ was the most agonizing aspect of His walk to the cross. This is the stage in which His blood was shed, and deliverance was received by those in chains. This is the stage in which His blood had to drip out of His body to fall on the ground in order to restore everything that came from the ground, and to purify all that was unclean. It was through His wounds and piercings that sicknesses and infirmities where cured.

Isaiah 53:5: *"He was wounded for our transgressions; he was crushed for our iniquities; upon him was the chastisement that brought us peace, and with his stripes we are healed."*

How can a single stripe heal the entire world? It was because He had done no violence, and no deceit came out of his mouth.

Colossians 1:13 *"He had delivered us from the domain of darkness and transferred us to the kingdom of His beloved son, in who we have redemption of sins."*

The soldiers who beat Jesus where demonstrating their physical ability to inflict pain. But Christ did not come to inflict pain on anyone; that is why He did not participate in what they were doing to Him.

These soldiers were challenging the peace Christ bought to the world. They were challenging the authority of Christ's resistance to physical battles. Despite all their attempts to provoke Him to call His angels and fight, He decided in His cautious mind to keep quit and continue to minister peace.

Ephesians 2:14: *"For he himself is our peace, who has made us both one and has broken down in his flesh the dividing wall of hostility."*

The walls that divided the people where broken through the flesh of Jesus and not through physical battles. When His flesh was broken, so were the walls of enmity, unfriendliness, war, arguments, debates, and fighting broken. The power of peace was demonstrated when Christ refrained Himself from fighting back against those who assaulted Him. Wars are ended by those who allow themselves to be beaten and carried away to be crucified. Peace is an individual experience that can be experienced through Christ in the midst of battles. Those who fight you are at the losing end, while you are empowered by the heavens into victory. You win spiritual battles by allowing yourself to lose physical battles. Christ allowed Himself to be called a loser in the battles of the flesh in order to be called victorious in the battles of the Spirit. When you fight a physical battle, you have lost a spiritual battle, and when you resist physical battles you overcome spiritual battles. The devil is depending on your aggression to gain strength so he can fight against your life. The strength that he uses against you is your own strength that you use when you become aggressive. He does not use one person's strength to destroy another, but he uses individual strength against each one of us …strength to dominate the body that provided him with that strength. This means that it is your attitude and character toward God's affairs that give the enemy a platform from which he can operate.

Matthew 26:51–52: *"And behold, one of those who were with Jesus stretched out his hand and drew his sword and struck the servant of the high priest and cut off his ear. There Jesus said to him, 'Put your sword back into its place. For all who take the sword will perish by the sword.'"*

Jesus rebuked one of His disciples and told him to put away the sword, because He understood that fighting physical battles would imply to God that they were now taking matters into their own hands, which was contrary to God's will and could have caused them to perish.

John 18:11: *"So Jesus said to Peter, 'Put your sword into its sheath; shall I not drink the cup that the Father has given me?'"*

This means that Jesus was aware of His standing with God. He knew that this was not how He should fight His battles; rather, it was the time to surrender Himself to the kingdom of darkness. Understand that the kingdom of darkness cannot contain a peaceful person without sin. Already Jesus had defeated evil, because He did not have an evil nature.

God is calling His church. It is time for us to put our physical swords into their sheaths and allow the will of God to prevail. In order to conquer the evil, we have to submit ourselves to the Lord and wear the amour of Christ to prepare for spiritual battles rather than physical ones.

Exodus 14:14: *"The Lord will fight for you, and you have only to be silent."*

Our physical and spiritual battles are all fought by the Lord, even though we sometimes don't see the spiritual ones. He fights and we see only the result. When you are physically approached by a witch, does that makes the battle more intense than when the witch attacks you spiritually? To God it does not matter how the witch comes to you, He continues to protect you. This should be your approach to faith. Therefore you must not feel safer only when you don't physically see an attack and feeling unsafe when you recognize an attack physically, to God there is no difference, and so should be your attitude.

God said in His word that He will fight for you against any nature of attack, whether an attack of sickness, threat, oppression, or interrogations. To Him these battles are the same, and He is able to protect you from any encounter you have with evil. Take your mind of those threats, and allow God hold your peace.

Philippians 4:7: *"And the peace of God, which surpasses all understanding, will guard your hearts and your minds in Christ Jesus."*

A man of war does not have peace within; this means that He does not have Christ.

John 14:27: *"Peace I leave with you; my peace I give to you. Not as the world gives do I give to you. Let not your hearts be troubled."*

When opposition arises and those who are against you are many, remember to keep the peace of Christ that He has left behind for you. Guard your heart and your mind in Christ Jesus, and do not fall into battles, for the peace of Christ is a powerful army. Use His peace to defend and defeat those seeking to destroy your life. The moment you allow your heart to be troubled is the moment your heart is exposed to attack. This will usher in fear, which will make you lose your faith, and when you don't walk by faith, God is not pleased. *"Do not fear those who kill the body but cannot kill the soul. Rather fear him who can destroy both the soul and body in hell"* (Matthew 10:28). For God has the final say on life and on death.

He is the one who possess the power to cast away all evil; therefore, do not fear the one who is limited and yet causes battles …someone who is man or woman like you, whose life is also in God's hands.

Second Kings 6:15–17: *"When the servant of the man of God rose early in the morning and went out, behold, an army with horses and chariots were all around the city. And the servant said, 'Alas, my master! What shall we do?' He said, 'Do not be afraid, for those who are with us are more than those who are with them.' Then Elisha prayed and said, 'O Lord, please open his eyes that he may see.' So the Lord opened the eyes of the young man, and he saw, and behold, the mountain was full of horses and chariots of fire all around Elisha."*

Elijah's servant could not see angels, but the time they were surrounded by an army with horses and chariots became the time for him to be uplifted. That situation made it possible for him to know the other side of God, and above all he was now able to see in the spirit just like his master.

Build your courage on God and pray as Elisha prayed for the servant—"O Lord, please open my eyes. Open my eyes, Lord, to see my solutions. Open my eyes, Lord, to see my breakthrough. Open my eyes, Lord, to see my successes and my uplifting … my promotion and my blessings. Open my eyes to see your angels all around me, taking charge of my problems. Open my eyes Lord to see the surroundings that possess my opportunities, places that I will be appreciated and accepted in order to make a greater impact here on earth..."

You are called by God, and your life must represent Him, meaning that you should not live in fear; rather, the Lord will bless you and give you peace (Numbers 6:24).

Psalm 44:3: *"For not by sword did they win the land, nor did their own arm save them, but your right hand and your arm, and the light of your face, for you delighted in them."*

You are God's delight. His right hand shall carry you through battles, and you shall hold your peace. His face shall shine on your paths and save you from many troubles. For it is not by the sword that you will win your battles; neither will it be by your own hand. It will be the peace of Christ that sustains and guards your mind in days of evil.

Sorrow Brings Goodness, Joy, and Happiness

Mark 14:32–34: *"And they went to a place called Gethsemane. And he said to his disciples, 'Sit here while I pray.' And he took with him Peter and James and John, and began to be distressed and troubled. And he said to them. 'My soul is very sorrowful, even to death. Remain here and watch.'"*

Isaiah writes about Jesus as a *"man of sorrow"* (Isaiah 53:3)

Christ did not bear His own sorrows; He bore the sorrows of the world. The extent of darkness that man lived in brought Him sorrow. The sorrows of man became His. Because of His passion to save souls and to rescue mankind, He was called "a man of sorrow." Surely He has borne our grief and carried our sorrows.

The pain that was meant for the world was now on His shoulders. The entire creation wanted to see how He would manage to carry the sins of the whole world on His shoulders and rescue everyone from the chains of evil. Many believed that was an impossible mission to perform, but to God it was a sacrifice that was not impossible to offer. When Christ came closer and closer to the cross, His soul began to sense all the troubles and afflictions, and every sin that had been committed by man on earth. All these were awaiting Him at the cross—the sins of the entire world on the shoulders of one man.

Christ became sorrowful for us so that we might receive the joy of the Lord.

John 16:20: *"Truly, truly, I say to you, you will weep and lament, but the world will rejoice. You will be sorrowful, but your sorrow will turn into joy."*

Sorrow introduces joy into our lives. Whenever you are sorrowful, rejoice, for the joy of the Lord has come.

John 16:21: *"When a woman is giving birth, she has sorrow because her hour has come."*

This means that sorrow comes along with happiness. When gifts of God are about to come into your life, that very hour is the hour of sorrow. Sorrow comes just for a while. It ushers in massive breakthroughs. To the spiritual man, Christ is saying that his sorrows will turn into joy. This is not a process, but a twist … a sudden turn. At the very hour you are in deep sadness, your sadness will turn into joy. At the very hour the devil ends your contract at work, and you hold those papers, spiritually you are signing a paper for a new job.

The moment you experience a loss, spiritually you experience gain. Does this make sense? No, it does not, but to God it does. You see, we cannot experience happiness all the days of our lives. That is why God allows sorrow just as you are uplifted. This is the love of God. His love allows sorrow for a moment and joy for a lifetime. This joy comes at the hour when you are supposed to endure sorrow.

Jeremiah 31:15–17: *"Thus says the Lord: 'A voice is heard in Ramah, lamentation and bitter weeping. Rachel is weeping for her children; she refuses to be comforted for her children, because they are no more.' Thus says the Lord: 'Keep your voice from weeping, and your eyes from tears, for there is a reward for your work,' declares the Lord, and they shall come back from the land of the enemy. There is hope for your future, declares the Lord."*

How must a mother behave after losing her children? Rachel wept and refused to be comforted. This is how a true mother would behave when her children have been butchered by the enemy in front of her. As Rachel was busy lamenting—at that very moment when she lost her children—lo and behold, the Lord appeared to her in her very hour of her weeping to bring good news to her. The question is, did God not know that Rachel's future was good? Why did He come at that particular time to meet her? The reason is that God's words of inspiration were set to be spoken at that particular time. That was the right time for God to encourage her. Her loss became key for her to have a visitation from her Maker. This means that she would not have been the mother of nations if she had not lost her first children, but now, because the Lord wanted to comfort her, He came with a higher blessing to encourage her. God did not say anything about her first children, meaning that they were not going to make her the mother of nations. But those that God said were coming became the chosen ones for greatness.

There is no need for you to claim what you have lost to the land of the enemy. What you need to do is just believe the word of the Lord that says, *"they shall come back"* and *"there is hope for your future."* Allow these words to have a permanent residence in your heart and in your mind. Convince yourself that God is speaking to you, and there is hope for your future. The extent of your hurt does not matter. God did not send angels to comfort Rachel, but He came personally to give her that word. He spoke them into her spirit to revive hope for her tomorrow.

Most people measure life with what happens to them today. Become unique; measure life from God. Hope is there for your future. Train your spirit to see emotional distress as a sign of joy and hope in His word.

Psalm 39:7: *"And now, O Lord, for what do I wait? My hope is in you."*

If God is assuring you of a bright future, what then will you still look for? Is God not the one who commands the winds to their direction and call stars by their names? When God is the last to speak, who else is that brave? The finger of the Lord has pointed your journey along His paths, and no one can mislead you.

Psalm 31:24: *"Be strong, and let your heart take courage, all you who wait for the Lord!"*

Mark 5:38–42: *"They came to the house of the ruler of the synagogue, and Jesus saw a commotion, people weeping and wailing loudly. And when he had entered, he said to them, "Why are you making a commotion and weeping? The child is not dead but sleeping.' And they laughed at him. But he put them all outside and took the child's father and mother and those who were with him and went in where the child was. Taking her by the hand he said to her, 'Talitha cumi,' which means, 'Little girl, I say to you, arise.' And immediately the girl got up and began walking (for she was twelve years of age), and they were immediately overcome with amazement."*

It is surprising to learn that the people who were weeping and wailing loudly now laughed at Jesus when He came to give them a solution. The very same people who gave up on the child laughed when someone came to lift up the child. The fact that they had never seen anyone speaking like Jesus did, did not mean that He did not know what He was talking about when He said, *"The child is not dead but sleeping."* This is how most of us behave when we are in distress; we laugh at the very same word that would give back that which we have lost. We laugh at the very men and women of God who carry the anointing to resolve our matters.

Even some men of God could have packed their bags and left the child when they were laughed at, ignoring what God said they should do, because some people who did not know the grace of God began to laugh at them. You see, if this is what you do as a believer, you will not touch lives. You will lose your focus, and you will raise no one. The difference between those who live by faith and those who don't is attitude. But there was those who were lamenting and at that moment began to encounter their miracle, in the midst of grief.

Romans 3:7: *"But if through my lie God's truth abounds to his glory, why am I still being condemned as a sinner? And why not do evil that good may come?"*

Receive the words of comfort that God's messengers carry to revive your spirit. If God is glorified, whether they are lies or not, what matters is that God's power has manifested. Why do we still condemn the very same help that God send into our lives?

Evil cannot by any means glorify Christ. Christ is glorified by what is good, and if what is a "lie" can glorify God, then let it be. God is calling you to a place where you can realize and accept the solutions He provides and appreciate all His ways, which are designed specifically for you so you can live a blessed life. Realize the ways that will resurrect your spirit, and begin to praise God for remembering you when you were in distress.

Despised To Have Long Suffering

Isaiah 53:3: *"He was despised … and we esteemed him not."*

The ministry of Jesus on earth was not respected by many, and some looked down on Him. The reason was that people never accepted Christ as their Messiah. They knew that the Messiah was coming, but they did not want the one who came. Maybe His stature and His appearance were not those of a Messiah, or maybe His behavior did not convince them that He was a Messiah.

Sometimes people look at how a person dresses, walks, or even where he lives before they can believe what that person claims he is. This means that there is a particular system on earth that deals with the minds of people against one another, especially those who do not have enough to sustain themselves. Christ might have been born from a poor home with not too many learned people around, and with little income to sustain the entire family.

Psalm 22:18: *"They divide my garments among them, and for my clothing they cast lots."*

To cast lots means to expect a certain outcome out of "mere chance." It was indeed a "mere chance" that some got to know this God. The actions of these soldiers paved the way for many to come into fellowship with Christ. Out of the mere chance of grace, many were chosen. No one can measure the amount of grace that leads people to Christ, and many did not acknowledge it. But despite that "mere chance", His grace is sufficient (2 Corinthians 12:9).

Ephesians 1:5–6: *"He predestined us for adoption as sons through Jesus Christ, according to the purpose of his will, to the praise of his glorious grace, with which he has blessed us in the Beloved."*

We did not choose Jesus, but He chose us (John 15:16). He loved us before we loved Him (1 John 4:10); and it is not by ourselves that we are saved, but by grace. Grace is a gift, it does not result from any work, lest any man should boast (Ephesians 2:8–9). Therefore, it does not lie entirely on you that you are now saved, but rather on the grace that by a "mere chance" you knew Christ when you nearly perished in a dreadful sickness, or a car crash. But thank God that, after you realized how life can end just like that, you gave your life back to Him and acknowledged what He has done for you out of mere chance. And you made it!

Casting lots gave a positive outcome to some. They gained something by chance. But to God there are no chances. It was through His will that you are saved. It was this unconscious act by these soldiers that gave many the portion of the garment of Christ and symbolized a breakthrough to many souls. The soldiers thought they were despising Jesus when they began to cut into pieces the clothes that He was wearing, not knowing that their acts was a prophetic symbol that signified a distribution of spiritual gifts, talents, and blessings to anyone who is willing to walk with Christ. This means that we all qualify to share in what Jesus had.

They did whatever it took to bring Him down to nothing. They took the covering of the Messiah and made fun of it. It was the same garment that one woman, who was troubled with an issue of blood, touched, and it did wonders for her. To other men it was just a cloth. The garment that some desired to put on for glorious manifestation became trash to others. This implies that Christ will become to you what you want Him to become.

The fact that you are a believer and you are despised does not mean you should begin to look down on yourself. Begin to look into the manner of Jesus. He was despised, and in the midst of it all, God used His garment as a symbol to bring victory to man. For the mere fact that people undermined the garment that Jesus was wearing did not change how God saw the garment. The power that was stored in it was still present, and it was upon the opportunity that man seized to tap into the anointing of Christ, through His garment. But what made the difference was how each one perceived it. That cloth was still the cloth of the Messiah no matter how they perceived it.

When people despise you to the point that they perceive you as nothing, do not be disheartened. Rejoice, for there is something God has placed in for you in that situation. You are talented, and people despise your talents. Rejoice, for God will use the very same people to advance your gifts. When those who perceive you as nothing talk of how low you are, fill yourself with hope and do not be dismayed.

The tongues of those who despise you shall call your name to the corridors of greatness. Sometimes people forget that each and every one of us has a different way of perceiving things. What you value, somebody might not value, and what somebody values, you might not value.

Therefore, those who see nothing in you will market your works with their own tongues. They will indirectly make people aware of your existence. They will realize after they have spoken that they have, in fact, lifted your name high. If you are gifted in the works of the hands, they will carry your product and criticize it, not being aware that they are marketing you for greater opportunities. This is what we may call, God's Free Marketing Network (GFMN). When you are despised, put into operation the fruit of long suffering. Through long suffering, you pass through situations that only God will allow you to pass through. When they despise your calling or whatever initiative you take, pray to God to develop that fruit. It is through long suffering that the Lord will make known to man the gifts He has given you for your life.

Romans 11:13–14: *"Now I am speaking to you Gentiles. Inasmuch then as I am an apostle to the Gentiles, I magnify my ministry in order somehow to make my fellow Jews jealous, and thus save some of them."*

The gifts of God over your life are just there to make others jealous in order for God to use you to win them over to His kingdom. Now, before some partake of God's kingdom, they first despise what you have. Besides that, the devil will try to prevent you from exercising what God has given you. Challenges of life will raise bars against the foundations of your belief, and if you are not well grounded in Christ, having long suffering, you won't be able to patiently endure what men say. These are the hindrances you might encounter, and if you are not focused you will stumble.

Therefore, put your focus on that which God has blessed you with to sustain your purpose and your mandate here on earth. If you do not know what God has given to you, create it. Create your purpose according to God's word, and you shall excel. It is through what God does through you that will make your accusers jealous and make them despise you.

Long suffering is an attribute that God has bestowed on each and every believer according to the measure of His will and purpose. Some people have decided to abandon their belief in Christ, simply because they could not endure the negative words spoken by people. This means that, to them, the words of man have more of an influence in their lives than what God says. And they themselves end up despising and discouraging those who managed to endure simply because they have occupied themselves and allowed the spirit that pulled them down to function also in their lives. It is not how low they look down on you that matters, but it is how high God has placed you that really matters in life.

God gives us projects to fulfill, but not all people delight in this. Some will discourage you and say things that will drain all the energy and vigor you once had. But God, who sees the end from the beginning, has prepared everything for you; all that you need to do is to be patient and endure. The Greek word for "long suffering" is *makrothumia*. It means being patient and loving in your relationships with others. It also means having a slow temper that causes you to delay reacting in anger. The term *long suffering* has nothing to do with suffering, but everything to do with love for others in times of difficulties, especially those who wrong you and those who see nothing good in you.

On the other hand, the Greek word for "patience" is *hypomone*, which means "to bear up under" and reflects the way you wait under different circumstances. It is only through God's spirit that, whenever you are wronged, you will be able to love back. Long suffering is the product of God's influence in your life. It is described as calmness and a state of content in times of difficulties. It reassures the love that God once offered through His son, Jesus. It puts into practice all that God has deposited in you, and it exposes the extent to which we ought to love those who despise us as they live in ignorance. And those who are God's children who do not live according to what people say should have the spirit of long suffering so they can answer the very same call Jesus came to earth for. Therefore, wait patiently on Him, who settles every dispute raised by the men who do not appreciate any work that is not done by them. The Lord is near, and every expectation you have will be met.

Prejudice for Selflessness

Matthew 27:20–21: *"Now the chief priests and the elders persuaded the crowd to ask for Barabbas and destroy Jesus. The governor again said to them, 'Which of the two do you want me to release for you?' And they said, 'Barabbas.'"*

Some people persuade others to destroy you while they themselves remain behind the scenes giving instructions. Sometimes the people who approach you with confidence to insult you and to demand things from you, especially in organizations or companies, are often not the real culprits. The same thing happened to Jesus; the chief priests and the elders were the ones who secretly influenced the crowd to ask for Barabbas to be released. The crowd just echoed what transpired behind the scene. Jesus was sentenced by the crowd and crucified by soldiers, but the chief priest and elders were the instigators of everything.

Jesus was unjustly convicted over Barabbas. According to the principles of prosecution, His trial was not fairly handled; rather, a notorious prisoner was released over Jesus because the crowd cried for the blood of Jesus. No one from the crowd came near to rescue Christ; everyone of them wanted Him crucified. There is really no comparison you can make between Jesus and Barabbas. But if Jesus was released, who would have become a sacrifice for mankind? Barabbas definitely was not the Savior, but he himself needed to be included in the grace of salvation that Jesus brought with Him. Otherwise, Barabbas became one of the people to experience the mercies of the Lord. He was not convicted for the crimes he committed, but he experienced forgives and was released, meaning that Jesus stood in the gap for him as well. The crowd believed that, through their injustices toward Jesus in favor of Barabbas, they were punishing Him, not knowing that they were helping Christ to fulfil the mandate, that was His purpose on earth.

There are moments in life in which people begin to draw a premature conclusion about you without having all the facts and evidence, just as Jesus was unjustly convicted with no facts or evidence to support His conviction. As a child of the most-high God, such things will be part of what you will go through, and you need to thank God for them.

Yes, it is not fair to carry somebody else's wrongs on your shoulders and take the blame, especially when you have done all that is humanly possible to do everything right on your behalf. God does not work with evidence or facts; He only does His will.

Proverb 16:9: *"The heart of man plans his way, but the Lord establishes his steps."*

No one wishes to fail, and we all desire good things for the future. Some will acquire success through evil routes, and some will acquire success by waiting on the Lord, but the fact of the matter is that all those men and women desire to be led to the future they planned. Before God establishes man, he exposes him to prejudice. He exposes him to wrongful verdicts and accusations in order to establish selflessness. He exposes him to the shame or prejudice in order to equip him with a grace of offering. It is through this grace of offering that God has instilled in you the desire to give back to His kingdom after He has established you. Prejudice affirms selflessness in the life of a believer.

Christ did not take any offence when Barabbas was chosen by the people over Him. To Him it was not a heartbreaking exercise, but an act of offering Himself to advance another. Are people advancing through what you have established? Are they elevated at your expense, while you are unfairly treated? Is there someone who is preferred over you at your company or in church? Or are you imprisoned for an act you did not commit while the perpetrator is free? Then rejoice, for there is a unique favor that moves through selflessness.

Second Timothy 2:15: *"Do your best to present yourself to God as one approved, a worker who has no need to be ashamed."*

Do not complain or be ashamed, for there is always a great reward for those who are selfless. Psalm 55:22: *"Cast your burden on the Lord, and he will sustain you; he will never permit the righteous to be moved."*

A selfless person has no burdens. Why? Because all his burdens are cast unto the Lord. Some people do not want to learn the art of giving; they even refuse to give their burden unto the Lord. Such people are not givers. They carry sickness, and they carry poverty and heavy loads. This is another aspect of giving and proves the point that only Jesus qualifies to take care of your needs. The moment you acknowledge Christ, you are introduced to the kingdom of givers. And the very same principle is applied in all walks of your giving, including giving away your burdens to God.

The Lord also sustains you. God does not sustain your burden, but He sustains you. He brings you to a point of self-realization—a point of being aware of your surroundings, and your surroundings becoming aware of you. If you are a believer and your surroundings do not feel your presence, you can easily be moved. Allow God to fill you with His weight to stay put, unshakable, unmovable, and not intimidated. A selfless person does not think of his own interest, but rather for the interests of others as well (Philippians 2:4). *"God is our refuge and strength, a very present help in trouble"* (Psalm 46:1). *"The Lord is my shepherd; I shall not want"* (Psalm 23:1).

If the Lord is present, what else do you seek? His presence comes with everything, but all that you have to do is to cast it all on Him, and He shall fill you up with His Spirit. He will supply all your needs according to His riches in glory by Christ Jesus.

Therefore, all these—prejudice, discrimination, injustice, inequality, intolerance, partiality, unfairness, and biasness—terminate destinies, but to a selfless person, they sharpen the art of perceptivity. And rejoice, for there is a great reward for you, the one who is discriminated against. Whoever bypasses you fraudulently on his way up, will also bypass you on his way down. Aspire to become selfless in the midst of prejudice, and the Lord will fill you up with His nature.

Save Yourself, with Meekness

Luke 23:35: *"And the people stood by, watching, but the rulers scoffed at him, saying, 'He saved others; let him save himself.'"*

There are situations in life in which people will do nothing but look aside when you are passing through tribulations of life. They watch on without doing anything to assist you. Those who speak are those who question your relationship with the Lord. These people have become spectators of your life as you pass through fire. They want to see if the Lord will really deliver you. *"He trusts in the Lord; let him deliver him"* (Psalm 22:8). They proclaim your trust in God and your delight in the King of kings, but because they are blind, they don't realize that they have just confessed what God will do for you, that is, when they proclaim that, "he trust in the Lord" and "Let him (God) deliver him" (psalm 22:8).

When it is your time to pass through afflictions, the only person you should walk with is Christ. Allow all others to be spectators; their work is to witness how God will deliver you. Jesus did not bother people when He was scoffed; He asked those who arrested Him to let His disciples go. Why? Because He understood that this was His situation and had nothing to do with His disciples.

Do you persistently bother people when things are tough in your life? Do you go around seeking answers and comfort from everyone when you are going through afflictions? Do you tell everyone your stories, looking for them to tell you what you want to hear? Look, give people their space; allow them to go. Kindly tell them that what you are going through is your own load to carry; no one will understand how to assist you in carrying it. Also, allow the scoffers to scoff, and the spectators to keep on watching.

When the soldiers came for Jesus, they interrupted His prayers in the Garden of Gethsemane and dragged Him to the cross. Not once did He stand up and seek help from any man. He asked the disciples to pray, and they were asleep. Well, that prayer was for them, and not for Him. They even fell asleep. But the point is that you should go alone and release the rest of the people. Enter the fire alone; call no one to enter with you.

Allow yourself to be ridiculed, for out of that situation, the grace of meekness will manifest allowing you to claim your earthly inheritance, assigned by Christ when He died on the cross.

Matthew 5:5: *"Blessed are the meek, for they shall inherit the earth."*

People watched as Christ was nailed on the cross, asking themselves so many questions, which they could not answer. Some were saying *"He cannot save himself"* (Matthew 27:42). These people did not know that there was no way Christ would save Himself, because He wanted to die, so that you and I could inherit the earth. They provoked Him to call His angels and perform a mighty miracle, but knowing the will of the Father, He submitted to death, so that He might rise in glory. He patiently looked on to generations of mankind, longing to give over His inheritance so His sons and daughters could possess the earth.

Do you want to possess the earth? Allow yourself to go alone to the cross with Christ Jesus, and let other people remain on the sidelines. By so doing, you shall inherit the earth and all that is in it. The meek find rest from the Lord.

Matthew 11:29: *"Take my yoke upon you, and learn from me, for I am gentle and lowly in heart, and you will find rest for your souls."*

It is one thing to put any yoke upon your shoulders, and it is another to take the yoke of Christ upon you. The Lord wants us to learn from Him how to be meek. Before Jesus spoke of meekness, He spoke of God hiding things from the wise and revealing His mysteries to little children. The reason for that is that God's kingdom is a kingdom that reflects the behavior of a child. Children are gentle and lowly at heart, and when you are like them you receive God's revelations, the hidden treasures of the God's kingdom.

This means that, when you accept Christ and you are lowly in heart, you receive the deep understanding of God's operation, and the hidden things are also revealed to you. These hidden things are the treasures of God's kingdom, and these are the gifts of the spirit. (1 Corinthians 12:7–10). These gifts are given to the lowly … the meek …those who depend on God for their next step. They are given to such people in order to shame the wise. Also, the meek and lowly receive the higher gifts (1 Corinthians 13:1–3)—speaking in tongues of men and angels, attaining prophetic powers, understanding all mysteries and all knowledge, and having all faith. These are the higher categories of spiritual gifts.

A lowly heart experiences an outpouring of love. Jesus had a lowly heart; hence, He walked in love. You cannot separate love from a lowly heart, as love resides from the heart. Meekness carries love within it and it also attracts higher spiritual gifts. It is up to an individual to allow the love that is found in a lowly heart to fade. Jesus wants us to learn from Him and to carry His yoke—the yoke of salvation. His yoke is the yoke of loving unconditionally all those who are our enemies who are seeking our downfall. In fact, a believer should not fear the enemy, for all his enemies are taken care of by Jesus. Our duty here on earth is to have a heart that resembles that of Christ. The people suggested to Christ that He should save Himself from the cross, and He did not comply, because the cross was His refuge for glory. People did not see the cross as a means of help for Jesus, because they were ignorant. To them there was no help for Him, but Christ knew He was nailed onto His help, and they did not perceive that.

Before He was nailed, the soldiers forced Him to carry His cross; in other words, He was forced to carry His own breakthrough. He did not want to let go of His elevation. He held tight to His cross, for through it, He would receive His glory. They thought there would be special help for Him, but little did they know that the cross was His special help.

In times of difficulty, distress, and trouble, listen not to those who say you must save yourself, for they do not see that you are saved already. That same cross that you are carrying is your breakthrough; refuse to throw it away. Learn from Christ and stay focused. Close your ears to the crowds, for they will disturb you. You know why Christ was crucified publicly before man? Because God wanted to prepare a decent table for Him. So shall the outcome of your afflictions be. Those gathered together discussing your suffering are strategically positioned to witness your breakthrough. It is from there that they will understand why you were lowly in heart when you walked through the fire. It is from there that they will begin to acknowledge what the Lord has done through your life. It is from there that they will bow down in awe to glorify the King of kings ... the performer of mighty works ... the one whose works cannot be understood by man ... who is the beginning and the end in every situation you encounter in life as you strive toward your destination.

Conclusion

Destiny Encountered

Proverbs 15:21: *"Folly is a joy to him who lacks sense, but a man of understanding walks straight ahead."*

Do you want to walk straight ahead in life, conquering every obstacle that wants you to deviate from your chosen path? If so, then seek understanding. Understanding is the knowledge to access a divine mandate on a particular matter. In other words, understanding is the ability to comprehend heavenly solutions. It provides answers to all things here on earth, above and below. It makes a wise man remain silent in disputes (Proverbs 11:12), simply because he knows the end result of the matter. Understanding governs the earth, and all principles of God revolves around it. It settles the differences between the poor and the rich. It offers peace and reconciliation to enemies, and it supplies man with sufficient ability to endure. A man of understanding lacks fear, for he understands how to gain boldness. He understands how to access his destiny and how to be established. He is aware of his surroundings, and all his plans succeed.

Proverbs 2:2: *"Making your ear attentive to wisdom and inclining your heart to understanding."*

Your ear should be attentive to wisdom, but though one can live without an ear, one cannot live without a heart, and that's where understanding resides. This means that, as much as your heart beats, so shall be the veins of your understanding. A deaf man can comprehend life principles, but a heartless man never lives. Trees and plants all breathe through the understanding of the Lord. Birds fly because the Lord understands that they cannot walk like man. All planets are carried by the Lord through understanding, and in the beginning, the Lord commanded them, and they began to revolve. The heart of man should incline to the path on which He walks. His understanding should always guard his actions. It should always act as a guide in all his ways (Proverbs 2:11; Proverbs 1:5).

Matthew 7:14: *"For the gate is narrow and the way is hard that leads to life."*

When you are a child of God, it can be difficult for you in life; you may be unable to get your breakthrough in all areas of your life. But begin to understand that you are on the road to life. This means you are on the right track. Why? Because the bible says so.

Jesus met a man who had been blind from birth. Jesus spat on the ground and made mud, and with this mud He anointed the blind man's eyes at the pool called Sent. And after the man was healed, the Pharisees began to question him. They questioned him because they were not pleased with the fact that his healing had taken place on a Sabbath. Then the man responded: John 9:25: *"One thing I do know, that though I was blind, now I see."*

Two major things happened before the blind man could testify. Firstly, Jesus anointed him (John 9:6). His anointing was very unique—it was not with oil but with mud made with Jesus's saliva. Biologically, saliva is used to soften food, and it also acts against irritants, substances that cause a continual distraction.

Secondly after the man was anointed, he was sent to the Pharisees to give testimony. The man, who knew nothing about the gospel, now was the minister of the word. The Pharisees even began to wonder if he was one of the disciples of Jesus (John 9:28), because of the manner in which he spoke. This man did not want to say anything except for what Jesus had done for him. The saliva of Christ had softened his vision to access divine mandate—understanding. Through the anointing of mud, the man began to act against the irritating Pharisees—the people who distracted his vision …the people who did nothing about his blindness. The people who did not have an understanding of how God works, Jesus answered: *"It was not that this man sinned, or his parents, but that the works of God might be displayed in Him"* (John 9:3).

The works of God were not displayed through the blind man; rather they were displayed in him. Hence, the Creator could work in a man in order to give him his sight.

There is only one thing you have to know, and that is to understand that God is at work in your life, because He is the only one who understand how to work within a person. Each and every single day—every hour, minute, and second—God is busy working on something in your life … adding and subtracting, calculating and analyzing every single step you intend to take. Most people cannot comprehend this. They think that, when they go through hardship, God has abandoned them. They assume that, when they do not see anything happening, God is not there. The Bible says, in John 9:1, *"As He [Jesus] passed by, he saw a man blind from birth."*

This man had not seen or heard of Jesus before, but his destiny had already been in place from birth. Nobody told him about Jesus and His healing powers; rather, Jesus was the one who saw him. Jesus is looking at you as well. You need not see Him, for He is the one looking at you, weighing your case … looking at how best can He bring reconciliation into your family, and how best can He revive your spirit, and how best He can bless you financially or restore your health.

Love is not love until you have an understanding of the love that Christ offered.

If you love without understanding that love, there will be many things you will miss along the way, and that love will one day disappear. Understand that every bad situation—at work, at home, in marriage, in business, at church, and everywhere else—is a good platform from which God can do something. Understand that the reason you exist is that God exists. The love that God has for you is immeasurable, and it cannot be compared with anything.

You cannot afford to panic when Jesus is around. Have that understanding. When you have gone through a lot in life and all your hope is gone and you have lost your trust in Him, just revive your understanding that everything that happens is for a good reason. Jesus is doing something, even if you do not worship Him the way you used to. He is doing something now, because He cares for you.

Even if we do not see the way, He is doing something new. Do not lose your understanding of the manner in which Christ works. That understanding will develop into trust, and when you have begun to fully trust in Him again, your faith will have been revived. People do not perish because they do not have faith; rather, they perish because they do not know (Hosea 4:6). But what good is the word of knowledge if it cannot be understood? We must have wisdom and understanding regarding the things that we know. Many people know that Jesus Christ is the Messiah, but they do not understand how to walk with Him. Because they do not understand, their knowledge does not become effective. Know and understand that all the trials you are going through in life are for a good cause.

The Lord is anointing you with mud. He is about to send you out with a word of testimony so that you can tell others of His goodness.

John 9:35–36: *"Jesus heard that they had cast him out, and having found him he said, "Do you believe in the Son of Man?" He answered, "And who is he, sir, that I may believe in him?""*

The blind man was restored and had nothing to say but to proclaim Jesus's miracle. The Pharisees wanted to use him against Jesus, and after they failed to get what they wanted from him, they chased him away.

The man did not go to look for Jesus, but the Bible says, *"Jesus heard … and having found him,"* which means that Jesus had been looking for him all along. You will never be outside of the mind of God. Even if man chases you away, He is there watching. In whatever state you find yourself, Jesus has been looking for you, and He has found you. Speak as the blind man did: *"And who is he, sir, that I may believe in him?"*

John 9:37: *"Jesus said to him, 'You have seen him, and it is he who is speaking to you...'"*